Flames Over New England

By Olga Hall-Quest
Flames Over New England
From Colony to Nation
The Bell That Rang for Freedom
Guardians of Liberty: Sam Adams and
John Hancock
With Stanley in Africa
Jamestown Adventure
Shrine of Liberty: The Alamo
How the Pilgrims Came to Plymouth

Flames Over New England

The Story of
King Philip's War: 1675-1676

OLGA HALL-QUEST

Illustrated by Christine Price

E. P. Dutton & Co., Inc.
NEW YORK

Contents

Northfield (Squakeag)

Dunstab

Deerfield R.

Peskeompscut

Millers R.

Mount Wachusett

Nashua R.

Deerfield

Nipmucks

Lancaster

Bloody Brook

Hatfield

MASSACHUSETTS BAY

Northampton

Hadley

Marlboro

Swift R.

Ware R.

Worcester

Blackstone R. (Pawtucket R.)

Chicopee R.

Menameset

Brookfield (Quabaug)

Mend

Westfield

Springfield

Simsbury

Windsor

Connecticut R.

Shetucket R.

Pa

Farmington R.

Hartford

RHO

Farmington

Wethersfield

ISLA

CONNECTICUT

Middletown

Mohegans

Narragans

Norwich

Quinnipiac R.

Wallingford

Haddam

Great Swamp Fig.

New Haven

Branford

Guilford

Saybrook

New London

Thames R. (Pequot R.)

Mystic R.

Stonington

Westerly

Lyme

LONG ISLAND SOUND

BLOCK ISLAND

Amesbury ⊙Salisbury
Haverhill⊙ ⊙Newbury
Rowley ⊙
⊙Ipswich
Merrimack R.
Andover ⊙Topsfield
⊙Wenham ⊙Gloucester
elms- ⊙Billerica
ford Salem
Woburn ⊙ Lynn Marblehead
Concord ⊙
Medford ⊙ ⊙Malden MASSACHUSETTS
Cambridge ⊙Charlestown BAY
Watertown⊙ ⊙Boston
Roxbury⊙ ⊙Hull
charles R. ⊙Hingham
Dedham ⊙ ⊙Cohasset ATLANTIC
field ⊙ Braintree⊙ OCEAN
⊙Weymouth ⊙Scituate
ham ⊙Marshfield

Duxbury⊙
⊙Attleboro Monponsett
Bridgewater⊙ ✕ Pond
Pawtucket Plymouth⊙
Taunton⊙ *Taunton R.* ⊙Middleborough
Rehoboth⊙ Squannakonk ⊙Assawompset Pond
Providence⊙ Swamp
Pawtuxet PLYMOUTH
Swansea Wampanoags CAPE COD BAY
⊙Wareham
Mount Hope ⊙Rochester ⊙Sandwich
✕Pocasset Swamp
Sakonnet R. Barnstable⊙ Yarmouth
⊙Portsmouth ⊙Dartmouth
AQUIDNECK
ISLAND BUZZARDS BAY
(Rh. Is.)
⊙Falmouth NANTUCKET
⊙Newport Little Compton SOUND
Sakonnet
Point
NARRAGANSETT
BAY
quamscut MARTHA'S
VINEYARD
NANTUCKET
ISLAND

New England 1675-1676

1 Land of Indians and English Settlers

Despite all the hardships and sufferings of that first winter on the wilderness shores of New England, the Pilgrims who had landed at Plymouth on December 11, 1620, had much to be thankful for. It had been their good fortune, first of all, to find a place to settle where no Indians lived. The Pawtuxets who had formerly occupied the site had been wiped out by a pestilence a few years earlier. And, along with their whitening bones, they had left behind cleared fields that stood ready to be taken over by the English.

There were many other Indians, though, along Cape Cod and Narragansett Bay, and in the interior, who were very much alive. While exploring Cape Cod, the Pilgrims had dodged a flight of arrows that confirmed their belief that the Indians were "readier to fill their sides full of arrows than otherwise." But instead of exterminating the handful of Pilgrims who survived that first rugged winter, as they could so easily have done, the natives came to help them.

On a day in March of 1621, a tall Indian, "stark naked, only a leather about his waist," walked boldly into Plymouth Town and called out cheerily to the startled Pilgrims, "Welcome, Englishmen!" He was Samoset, sagamore of a tribe that lived in an area on the northeastern coast that became the state of Maine. He had become friendly with English fishermen who had been coming there for years, and had learned their language.

Now Samoset was visiting the Wampanoags, and having satisfied his curiosity about the white newcomers and accepted them as friends, he returned to Plymouth a few days later with some of Chief Massasoit's warriors. It was on his third visit that he brought the young Indian who did so much for the Pilgrims that William Bradford called him a "special instrument of God for our good."

This Indian was Squanto, the lone survivor of the Pawtuxet tribe. Just prior to the outbreak of the pestilence, he had been kidnaped by an English shipmaster who intended to sell him and nineteen others as slaves in Spain. But Squanto escaped, eventually reached England, and was later sent by a London merchant to Newfoundland. Taken on there as an interpreter by a shipmaster bound for New England, he finally made his way back to his old home, only to find that it was nothing but a graveyard—that all that remained of his people were their bleached bones.

After his introduction to the English by Samoset, Squanto felt that he had come home again. He liked the Pilgrims so much that he spent the rest of his life with them. And what he did for his new friends, for these white men in an alien land, was of inestimable value to them. Having learned their language, he could converse with them and serve them as an interpreter. With Squanto as their guide, the Pilgrims soon became familiar with the Indian trails that threaded the surrounding forests. From him, they learned where and how to catch fish, how to tread eels out of mud, and what greens and herbs in the deep woods were edible. The Indians' greatest gift to the white men was corn, and it was Squanto who taught them how to cultivate it as the natives did, in six-foot squares with the earth heaped up in the middle and fertilized with a dead fish or two.

There was another memorable March day in the spring of 1621 when Squanto accompanied Massasoit on his first visit to Plymouth. After ceremonious greetings and a venison feast, the Wampanoag chieftain and Governor John Carver smoked a pipe of peace, and concluded a treaty of friendship and alliance that was never broken during the lifetime of the great sachem. It was a treaty that worked to their mutual advantage. The Wampanoags had been considerably reduced in numbers by the pestilence, and they needed the protection of English firearms to intimidate their powerful enemies the Narragansetts, who had escaped the ravages of the plague. And certainly the young colony needed the good will of the Wampanoags. In addition to all the practical advantages of the alliance on both sides, there was genuine friendship between Massasoit and the Pilgrim leaders.

In welcoming and accepting as friends the first white men to settle permanently in New England, the Wampanoag sachem and his people could not foresee that the English were but the forerunners of what would be a steady stream of emigration from England. Just a decade after the Pilgrims founded their colony, the Puritan migration to Massachusetts began, and some twenty years before Massasoit's death, there were four separate colonies in the area of southern New England. Whatever the old chief may have thought of this influx of Englishmen, and the eventual effect it would have upon the natives of New England, he remained stanchly loyal to the Pilgrims who had broken ground and paved the way for those who came after them.

By 1675, Plymouth Colony included all of what is now southeastern Massachusetts, and had a population of about 5,000. Besides the original town of Plymouth that was still its capital, there were many villages and towns that had been settled in other parts of the colony. To the north of Plymouth were Duxbury, Marshfield, and Scituate, and southward, along the bay side of Cape Cod, were Sandwich, Barnstable, Yarmouth, and Eastham.

A short distance to the southwest of Plymouth was Middleborough, which had been the Indian village of Nemasket before its purchase by the English. The center of Middleborough was near the old "Wading Place" on the Nemasket River, across which all travelers between Plymouth and Massasoit's country had to pass. Nearby were the farming communities of Taunton and Bridgewater, and the most distant outpost settlements were Dartmouth to the south and Swansea and Rehoboth to the southwest.

Plymouth was still a struggling little colony with only about 300 settlers when the great Puritan migration to Massachusetts began in 1630. It was happy to have these strong Puritan neighbors, and proud, too, as Bradford said, "to have lit the candle that had lighted a thousand others." Soon the Pilgrims were driving their cattle to market in the neighboring colony to the north along the old Indian trail from Plymouth to Boston. This earliest of all roads made by the white man in America was known as the Bay Path.

Massachusetts became the largest and the most prosperous of the four colonies, and in 1675 there were about 17,000 people living in the colony, which had

expanded to include more than fifty towns. Within a
radius of twenty miles of Boston, the thriving seaport
and center of government, were a score of settlements
along the coast and in the bottom lands of the Charles,
the Concord, and the Neponset rivers—Dedham, Watertown, Medford, Malden, Sudbury, Concord, Bil-
lerica, and others. Farther west, Dunstable, Groton,
Lancaster, Marlborough, Mendon, and Wrentham
were strung out in a line running from north to south,
and beyond, far out in the Nipmuck country, were
the two isolated settlements of Worcester and Brookfield. Several small communities had also grown up
along the Connecticut River where it passed through
Massachusetts, of which the most important was
Springfield.

South of the Massachusetts border the great river
flowed down to its mouth through the colony of Con-
necticut. Early in the century, the Dutch from New
Netherland discovered and explored the Connecticut
River, and some years later built a trading post at
Hartford. But they were driven out of the valley by the
English, and groups of Puritans from Massachusetts
Bay trekked in, some of them settling at Hartford,
and others establishing communities at Wethersfield
and Windsor.

These towns formed the independent Commonwealth of Connecticut, separate from the colony of
New Haven to the west, which was also settled by
Massachusetts Puritans. In 1665, the two colonies
united, and as the Puritan colony of Connecticut be-

came the second largest of the four New England colonies, with a population numbering about 10,000, and with Hartford as the seat of government.

From the beginning, the Pilgrims had been Separatists—separated from the Church of England—and had established Congregational churches in their new homeland. Each church was independent, the congregation having the right to choose its pastor and elders, and other church officers. The meetinghouse, as the church was more often called, was a plain, unadorned structure in which there was no ornamentation—no stained-glass windows, no silver communion plate, no organ, no altar, and no candles. The simple Congregational service consisted of Bible reading, a sermon, and spontaneous prayer—that is, there was no Book of Common Prayer.

The Puritans were not Separatists when they emigrated from England. They had wanted to purify, or reform, the Anglican Church, and for that reason were called Puritans. After they settled in Massachusetts Bay, they adopted the Congregational form of worship, and the Pilgrims helped them organize a Congregational church. But the Puritans became the dominant group, ruled by strong-minded men who were determined to maintain the purity of God's commonwealth.

For they had entered into a covenant with God "to live as members of a holy society," based on the pattern laid down in the New Testament. They acknowledged no other will but that of God, and their lives were regulated by His will as it was expressed in the Bible. Since the Puritan clergymen were the interpreters of God's will for the individual and the community, they were an influential group. And they were highly educated men, most of them having graduated from English universities. That Massachusetts Bay had set up schools and Harvard College within ten years after its founding was mainly owing to the promotion of learning by its clergymen. One reason for their interest in education was to foil "that old deluder Satan" in his desire to "keep men from knowledge of the Scriptures."

Satan also kept them busy trying to protect Massachusetts from corruption. There were, for example, the religious dissenters who were often a trial, and against whom stringent laws were passed. Although the Puritans left England chiefly because the Anglican Church frowned upon their beliefs, they were themselves intolerant of religious differences.

The earliest, and the most famous, of the dissenters to disturb the peace of the holy society in the Bay Colony was Roger Williams. He had himself been harassed in England for his religious convictions, and in 1631 he accepted an invitation to serve the church in Salem, Massachusetts. Williams was a kind and gentle man, possessed of considerable charm and magnetism of personality, but he was also an unorthodox religious zealot.

Almost at once upon his arrival in Massachusetts, he incurred the hostility of the Puritan leaders, and of the clergymen particularly. The Boston church, he charged, was not sufficiently separatist; and the power of the magistrates, he insisted, should be limited to civil matters—they should have no authority to punish people for breach of the Sabbath or other religious offenses.

Having been made unwelcome in Massachusetts, Roger Williams went to Plymouth, where he joined the church and was invited to preach. Governor William Bradford described him as a man "godly and zealous, having many precious parts but very unsettled in judgment." Even the more tolerant Pilgrims could not accept his "strange opinions," and when Williams declared that the king had no right to grant charters to the colonies because the Indians were the real owners of the land, the Massachusetts General Court ordered him deported to England. He escaped into the wilderness, where he was befriended and sheltered by the Narragansett Indians, and in the spring of 1636 Williams purchased land from them at the head of Narragansett Bay for a settlement. He named it Providence in gratitude for his survival, and decreed that here no man would be molested because of his religion, whatever it might be.

There were other dissenters, particularly Baptists and Quakers, who, having been banished from Massachusetts, flocked to join Williams in his colony, called Providence Plantations. Another group settled the town of Portsmouth at the northern end of Aquidneck Island in Narragansett Bay, and soon afterward

Newport was planted at the southern tip of the island, and Warwick on the mainland south of Providence. For some years these towns were independent of one another, but continual strife finally forced Roger Williams to go to England to apply for a charter that would unite them, and in 1644 they became the Colony of Rhode Island, "a nest of pestilential heretics," in the eyes of all good Puritans.

In 1675, the colony was populated by something under 4,000 people, many of them Quakers, a sect that was especially obnoxious to the Puritans. Newport was the capital, and Williams, now an old man in his seventies, still lived at Providence and took an active part in the affairs of the colony.

Since Rhode Island was looked upon as a sanctuary "for every false doctrine that stingeth like a viper," it was not considered worthy of membership in the New England Confederation, which had been organized in 1643 by representatives from the three Puritan colonies of Massachusetts Bay, Plymouth, and Connecticut. Meetings were held periodically, and in turn, at the capitals of Boston, Plymouth Town, and Hartford, at which two commissioners from each colony consulted, and often took action, upon mutual problems.

Even under the harsh conditions and the isolation of pioneer life in the wilderness, the New England colonists prospered. Scorning indolence and ease, they worked hard and became successful farmers, tradesmen and businessmen.

The little one-room dwellings of an earlier day could still be seen in towns and villages, but by 1675 more commodious houses had been erected. Typically, they were two-storied houses with a loft above. They were built of oak and pine around a great central chimney, and covered outside with split-cedar clapboards. The second story projected over the lower, or ground, story, and for the casement windows small leaded, diamond-shaped panes were used. Left unpainted, the houses weathered to varying shades of gray and brown. They stood in the midst of gardens and orchards, and every house had a well, either with a rope and bucket or a long well sweep. Every house had a barn and sheds nearby, too, for the livestock, and some distance away were the cultivated fields.

Prosperity and growth were also reflected in the specialized services and industries that had opened up in the towns. There were carpenters, bricklayers, blacksmiths, millers, brewers, and cobblers. Each town had its sawmill, gristmill, and brewery. Upon the coast there were saltworks, and in some towns fulling mills for finishing homespun and home-woven cloth. And at Taunton, Saugus, and Braintree, ironworks produced the bar iron that was wrought into nails, anchors, chains, skillets, kettles, and other useful articles.

At first, most inland travel between towns was by foot or on horseback along the trails that connected them. But over the years these paths had been broadened and could now be used by two-wheeled oxcarts.

Small boats—ketches, sloops, and shallops—plied the rivers and coastal waters, bringing local products and manufactured goods from abroad to towns and settlements located on New England's waterways. The most profitable trade for the colonies developed when larger and sturdier cargo vessels were built and when venturesome seamen, putting out from the ports of Boston, Marblehead, Newport, and New London, sailed to the islands of the West Indies. Here the sugar planters were happy to trade for New England's products—for lumber and oak pipe staves, and for corn, salt fish, and pickled beef and pork.

In little more than a half century, the English settlers had made remarkable progress in establishing themselves in a hostile land, perhaps beyond their most hopeful dreams. But they had done no more than penetrate the wilderness. It was still there in a vast expanse of forests and swamps and streams. And it was crisscrossed by trails unknown to the Englishmen, for large areas were occupied by the Indians.

The various tribes of southern New England could understand one another, for all of them belonged to the Algonquian language group. It has been estimated that in 1674 there were some 5,000 Narragansetts. This largest and most powerful tribe occupied the territory between the Quinebaug River and the western shore of Narragansett Bay. To the northwest, in an area extending from Northfield, Massachusetts, south and east into Connecticut and Providence Plantations, were the villages of about 3,000 Nipmucks. In southeastern Connecticut, the Mohegans, and the Pequots they had absorbed, may have numbered about 2,500, and on Mount Hope Peninsula the Wampanoags added up to something over 1,000.

The Massachuset Indians, from whom the Bay Colony took its name, had been greatly reduced by wars and pestilence, and the remnant of this tribe, along with the Nausets, had been converted to Christianity, and lived in villages on Cape Cod.

The Pequots had been a warlike tribe who, under their sachem Sassacus, had got into trouble when they refused to surrender the murderers of two English traders—John Stone and John Oldham—to Massachusetts Bay for trial and punishment. Captain John Endecott was sent out with forty men on a punitive expedition, but did nothing more than stir up the Pequots by burning some of their lodges. When, early in 1637, the Indians began to vent their fury upon the valley settlements of the English, Connecticut appealed to the Bay Colony for help.

Joined by some of the Narragansetts, a Massachusetts force under Captain John Underhill, and a Connecticut contingent under Captain John Mason, attacked and set fire to the Pequot stronghold near the mouth of the Mystic River, and destroyed between 500 and 700 Indians. Sassacus fled to the Mohawks, who murdered him, and the Pequot prisoners were enslaved. Most of those who escaped death or capture took refuge with the Mohegans. This infuriated the

Narragansetts, and when they attacked the Mohegans, and were defeated by them, the New England Confederation became involved in bitter Indian rivalry. War was finally averted, and the Narragansetts were persuaded to keep peace with the other Indian tribes of New England.

The Algonquians were not nomads. They were agricultural tribes who tilled their cleared fields, and made some provision for the winter by storing surplus corn and dried fish in covered pits. Each village belonged to the tribe, and the land was held in common by the group. It was not unusual for the entire village to move to another location—where the hunting and fishing were better or where there was protection from winter winds in some sheltered valley. Occasionally the huts became infested with an "abundance of fleas," and then the Indians would "remove on a sudden" to a more comfortable site.

The tribe was ruled by a chief sachem whose counselors were the lesser sachems and sagamores. The position of the supreme leader was not held exclusively by men. The Pocassets and Sakonnets, small tribes subordinate to the Wampanoags, were ruled respectively by the squaw sachems Weetamoo and Awashonks. And Quaiapen, known as the Old Queen or "saunk squaw," was one of the lesser sachems of the Narragansetts.

The New England Indians did not have a body of religious beliefs nor did they worship a "Great Spirit." Having some idea of a spirit world, however, they believed in good and evil spirits. Their medicine men claimed to be able to control or propitiate the bad spirits by offerings, charms, and incantations. The Algonquian had not developed any idea of future rewards and punishments, but he may have believed in some vague form of life after death.

According to the 1628 charter of Massachusetts Bay, the "principal end of this Plantation" was "to win the natives of the country to the knowledge and obedience of the only true God and Savior of mankind." But most of the Puritan settlers, including the clergy, looked down upon the Indians as heathen of a subhuman species, and took no interest in saving their souls.

The Reverend John Eliot was one of the few who pitied the "poor Indians," who saw them as human beings with souls to be saved, and whose desire was "to make the name of Christ chief in these dark ends of the earth." The "somber, stocky man in black" began his labors in the early years of the Bay settlement. He took into his house at Roxbury, Massachusetts, where he was pastor, first one and then another young Indian who could speak and read English, and with their help mastered the Algonquian tongue. It was the Reverend Eliot who preached the first Protestant sermon to the Indians in their language on the North American continent.

Then, with the zeal of the dedicated missionary, he gathered his Indian converts together and settled them in the town of Natick on the Charles River. Here, a fort, a meetinghouse, and shelters for about 800 inhabitants were built under supervision by the Indians themselves, who were called "Praying Indians." Funds from England helped to pay for their food, clothing, and implements, and Natick became a successful demonstration of what could be done with Christianized Indians. By 1675, there were several thousand of them living in fourteen communities in New England.

Meanwhile, the Reverend John Eliot had undertaken the monumental task of translating the Bible into the Algonquian language. After ten years of labor, during which time he continued to look after his converts with the assistance of Captain Daniel Gookin, the "Apostle to the Indians" completed the crowning achievement of his life—*Mamusse Wunneetupanatamwe Up-Biblum God* (The-whole Holy His-Bible God).

Most of the colonists looked on the Praying Indians with distrust, and scoffed at their piety, declaring that it was a hypocritical way of earning an easy living. But, obviously, Christian dogma was beyond the grasp of these backward natives. Simple goodness they could understand, though, and they responded to the kindness not only of the Reverend John Eliot of the Bay Colony but also to that of the Reverend Samuel Treat and the Reverend John Cotton of Plymouth Colony, who also preached in their villages and made converts. There were obvious material advantages in becoming a Praying Indian, but these natives were grateful for something more, and most of them remained loyal to the colonists when the inevitable conflict between a civilized race and a primitive one erupted in a tragic war.

The great majority of New England's Algonquians not only spurned the Christian Indians as renegades but also felt a deep resentment toward the white man for imposing his religion and culture upon them. It was one of the most aggravating causes of mounting friction, for it was an intolerable insult to the Indian's pride in his own race. Old Chief Massasoit had looked upon the missionaries with such suspicious distaste that he had banned them within his territory in his early treaty with Plymouth Colony. Philip, who later became the Wampanoag sachem, was even more bitter and hostile toward them. In a chance encounter with Eliot, he twisted a button on the apostle's coat and said scornfully, "For your Gospel I care no more than for this button."

Even those Indians who would have none of the white man's religion were compelled by law to observe the Puritan code of behavior. Severe punishment was meted out to them, as well as to the colonists, for blasphemy or for speaking irreverently of God and the Christian religion. Plymouth strictly forbade the Indians to fish, hunt, plant, or carry burdens on the Sabbath. In Connecticut one of them was fined for traveling from Springfield to Hartford on the Lord's day, and another for firing a gun. On one rare occasion, two sachems, having been warned not to do unnecessary work on the Sabbath, poked a bit of sly humor at the Massachusetts General Court. "That will be easy," they said, "since we haven't much to do on any day."

The Indians had no political rights, and there were special laws that applied to them but not to the white men. They could not buy a horse without a permit. The only kind of boat they were allowed to own was their primitive canoe. And they had not been permitted to buy or own firearms until 1665—a permission that was withdrawn whenever the colonists feared there was danger of an uprising.

Although the Indians were treated as a subject race, the English courts made an effort to render justice to them. They sometimes served on juries that tried their own people, and they could bring complaints and grievances against the colonists, who were themselves punished as severely as the Indians when they were the offenders against the natives. And an effort was made to protect them from the harmful effects of drinking. It was the white man's liquor that the Indians tasted for the first time, and they quickly developed a thirst for it. The English passed a law that made it illegal to give or sell liquor to a native; that an attempt was made to enforce it is proved by the frequency with which mention of the offense appears in court records.

It was serious enough for the Algonquians that their way of life was being slowly undermined by the colonists who now regarded them contemptuously as lazy, dirty, and treacherous savages. It was even more serious for them that their forest holdings were being steadily diminished by the relentless encroachments of the white settlers. Whereas in earlier years they had traded with the Indians for food, furs, and wampum, now land was all that the English wanted from the natives. Land, Roger Williams observed, had become "one of the gods of New England."

Governor Josiah Winslow of Plymouth declared that the English did not possess "one foot of land" in the colony that had not been acquired "by honest purchase" from the Indians. And, with the few exceptions of fraud, this was true. The Pilgrims did not buy the original site on which they settled because all the Pawtuxets, except Squanto, who had formerly occupied it were dead. Purchase of other land from Indian owners, or those who claimed it, was strictly regulated by a law that required a permit from the government even before bargaining began. The Indians could keep their land if they did not wish to part with it, and, in their interests, the government forbade the sale or purchase of certain tracts, such as Mount Hope and "several other necks of the best land in the colony."

It would seem that the colonists got much the better bargain in giving the Indians woolen matchcoats (like the mackinaw jacket), cloth, axes, hoes, and kettles in exchange for their hunting grounds. But the natives wanted articles of English manufacture as much as the white men wanted their land. And some purchases were paid for in English pounds. Taunton, for example, paid Philip the not insignificant sum of £190 in 1672 for a four-mile tract.

It is probably true that many Indians did not understand the meaning of ownership of land as the English understood it. Since Indian villages and hunting grounds were owned in common by all the members of a tribe, it would not have been easy for them to understand how the sale of a tract could give the individual exclusive rights to the property he bought. Whether understood or not, the Indians frequently intended to continue hunting or fishing or gathering rushes on their former lands after the English had taken possession and moved in.

Basically, it was the coming of a strong, civilized people to their New England wilderness that spelled tragedy for the Algonquians. The white settlers who had moved into the territory did not doubt that they had a right to be there; in addition, they believed it to be their duty to impose their culture upon the primitive natives. On the other hand, the products of the advanced race were an irresistible lure for the Indians. In replacing their traditional weapons, clothing, tools, and utensils with those of English manufacture, they became ever more dependent upon the white men. And in their eagerness to trade with the newcomers they willingly bartered away the land that gave them a living.

To the self-righteous Puritans, God had given them this land of "the heathen people," as one of their clergymen said, "for a rightful possession."

2   White Man's Rule

On an April morning in 1671, a large gathering had assembled on the green at Taunton in Plymouth Colony. Governor Thomas Prence himself was there, along with other Plymouth officials, and representatives of the Massachusetts Bay Colony. Every man was armed with a musket and, at his side, a long sword that hung down below full knee breeches.

As the men moved restlessly about, they turned

often to look toward the south. When the sun had
climbed past the point of midmorning, Governor
Prence said irritably: "We can never depend on Philip.
It seems we'll have to go look for him. He is either
loafing along the way or sulking in his lodge."

But the governor was mistaken, for presently two
Indian warriors appeared and informed the Englishmen that their chief was waiting at Two-Mile River
for the governor of Plymouth to come to him. Out-
raged by what seemed to be the insolence of the Wampanoag sachem, Governor Prence dispatched his own
messengers to tell Philip that he should come at once
to Taunton Green, the place they had agreed upon for
the meeting. A few miles from Taunton, the English
messengers found the sachem and his warriors loung-
ing at ease along the banks of the river and under the
trees.

There were seventy tall, well-formed, copper-
skinned Indians in the group, most of them young.
The older men wore their straight black hair either
hanging loose or in two long plaits, but on most of
the younger ones it was closely cropped along the sides
of the head and worn in a high crest, or roach, on top
from front to back, and with an eagle feather stuck
in it. Except for a breechclout of deerskin and the
moccasins on their feet, they were naked.

King Philip, as the English called him, was probably
about thirty years old. It was easy to recognize him
as a chief by the proud lift of his head and the imperious glance of his black eyes. He was as tall, as

well proportioned, and as strong as the handsomest of his warriors. Besides the eagle feather, he wore a wampum headband and a belt of wampum, rich in intricate designs made with the shell beads that the Indians valued so highly.

Upon the approach of the two English messengers, the Wampanoags quickly rose to their feet and stood together, each holding his gun. Some of them also carried bows and arrows, but, having been permitted to trade with the white man for firearms and ammunition, they now preferred the Englishman's musket to their traditional weapons.

It was their sachem that the messengers questioned. Why had he stopped here at Two-Mile River? Had he not promised to be in Taunton before the sun was high? The young chief ignored the questions. He merely said, quietly and with dignity, "I am here. Let your governor come to me."

It was not the first time he had been summoned for a conference with the Plymouth authorities. It had happened in 1662 soon after he succeeded his brother as chief of the Wampanoags. At that time Philip received a curt summons to appear before the General Court to answer charges of disloyalty to Plymouth Colony—to be questioned about an alleged conspiracy between the Wampanoags and the Narragansetts. He denied it, and upon renewing the treaty of 1621 was allowed to depart.

Again, in 1667, Philip was accused of plotting against the English: this time of conspiring with the

French and the Dutch. Failing to find any evidence of a plot, the Plymouth Government was forced to drop the charges. Now, four years later, Philip had been called for yet another interrogation, and he knew that he would hear the ugly word "conspiracy" again. He knew, too, how hard it was not to become confused when the English pressed him for answers to their questions.

He was in no hurry to face the ordeal. Finally, after a long pause, he asked the impatient messengers, "How many men in Taunton?"

Sensing that Philip was suspicious, the Englishmen suggested that they remain at Two-Mile River as hostages with some of his men. And to this the sachem agreed. Then he walked rapidly on toward Taunton with all his warriors except the three who were left behind with the messengers.

But when he reached Crossman's Hill, a vantage point from which he had a clear view of the armed Englishmen pacing on Taunton Green, Philip halted. Having surveyed the scene, he continued on down to the mill nearby. Here it again seemed fitting that the governor should come to him. And he sent one of his men to Governor Prence to say, "Philip waits for you at Crossman's Mill."

The Plymouth officials were already angered by the delay. Now they clamored to go out and bring the sachem in forcibly. But the Massachusetts delegates advised against such rash action. They were there at the Wampanoag chief's insistence to see that he was given fair treatment. It was with the Plymouth authorities that he was in trouble.

At last Philip was persuaded to come in with his warriors. He had been assured that they would be allowed to sit together in the meetinghouse that faced the green and that all the guns of both the white men and the Indians would be stacked outside. When the conference began, the Englishmen in their dark suits sat on the wooden benches on one side of the aisle, and the naked Indians sat across from them.

The accusations and the questioning began. "We know that you are making preparations for war, Philip," the governor said. "We have learned on good authority that you are collecting arms, sharpening your knives and grinding your hatchets. We have seen the important men of other tribes on the trails that lead to your seat. Can it be, as we have heard, that you intend to attack your English friends?"

The question might not have been asked for all the attention Philip paid to it. Sitting with his interpreter before Governor Prence at the conference table, he said bluntly: "The English do harm to my planting lands. Your cows, your horses, and your pigs trample my corn."

It was a complaint that the Plymouth authorities heard often. And it was true that the livestock of the settlers did much damage to the Indians' unfenced cornfields. In that year of 1671, the officials of Plymouth Colony had to appoint committees in eleven towns "to view the damage done to the Indians by the horses and hogs of the English." The town of Rehoboth, which adjoined Wampanoag country, was the worst offender. But the English tried to be fair. Not only had Rehoboth been repeatedly fined; it had also been ordered to pay the Indians for damages to their crops and to build fences around their fields at the town's expense.

Impatiently, the governor reminded Philip of all this. "You know we listen to your complaints," he said, "and that we try to treat you justly. You know, too, that the English are your friends. But are you treating them as friends, Philip? Why do you make preparations for war?"

The sachem knew that he would be cornered. Already he felt confused and fatigued by the white man's talk. But he tried one more dodge. "I get ready to fight the Narragansetts," he explained.

"You do not," the governor said with accusing emphasis. "There has long been peace between you and your old enemies. And now it looks as if there were a conspiracy afoot. I have witnesses here who can tell you when and where they have seen you with the Narragansett sachem and important men of the tribe. We have the evidence that proves you are guilty."

Philip had learned what it meant when the words "conspiracy" and "evidence" were put together. He had also learned that the easiest way to get out of a corner into which he had been pushed was to confess. That was another English word with which he had become familiar.

So the Wampanoag sachem looked innocently at Governor Prence, and said: "I confess I do wrong. I conspire against the English who are my friends."

The men of Plymouth were satisfied. The delegates from Massachusetts had made no protest, for they had seen that the examination of Philip was conducted fairly. They were in agreement, too, with the articles of "submission" that the governor and his assistants now wrote out. In their words, Philip admitted "from his own naughty heart" that he had plotted against the English. He repented, and wished to declare anew his loyalty to the English Crown and to Plymouth Colony. And he promised to deposit all his firearms with the Plymouth authorities as security for his future good behavior.

It came as a shock to the Wampanoag chief to hear that he must hand over his guns to the English. He could see the sullen resentment in the eyes of his warriors, and for a moment he felt suffocated by his own anger. This had not happened before. On other occasions he had simply been reproved and dismissed. He knew, though, that he was trapped. He knew, too, that this was not the time to take his revenge.

Philip quickly recovered his composure. He took the quill pen that the governor handed him and signed the agreement with a large capital P. Some of the sagamores came forward, too, and put their marks upon the paper that was dated April 10, 1671.

The sachem led his men back to his seat on Mount Hope. The young warriors were in a rebellious mood.

Their guns had been taken from them for no good reason that they could see, and their chief had been humiliated. "Let us make war against the English now," they urged. "They treat us like dogs. Soon we will be nothing but their slaves."

Philip's anger had cooled. Back in his native forest he could think clearly again. Here he regained his courage, and the dignity and pride of his high position. Here he was the great sachem of a great people, and he could quickly forget the silly promises the men of Plymouth had forced him to make. He did not forget the humiliation, though. That was a slow burning in his breast. To his impatient warriors, he said: "The time is not now. We are not ready."

Although the talk was of war, there was peace on this April day on Mount Hope Peninsula (by its Indian name, Pokanoket), which extended into Narragansett Bay. Here at the north end, the Wampanoags had their chief village, and here Philip resided on top of the beautiful hill with the English name of Mount Hope. From a height of about 200 feet, he could look out over swamps and woodlands and streams into Rhode Island.

The lodge in which King Philip lived with his wife and young son was like all the other huts except that it was larger. The construction of the Wampanoag wigwams, like that of the other Indian tribes in southern New England, was simple. Flexible green saplings were planted in the ground and bent over to give the dwellings a rounded shape. Then they were covered with bark and reed mats sewn together with hemp. A hole was left in the top through which smoke could escape from the fire on a hearth in the center of the wigwam. There were usually two openings to catch the breeze whichever way it might blow. Around the interior walls was a low platform that served as both bench and bed for the inmates. It was the kind of shelter that met the Indians' simple needs, and one that could easily be transported elsewhere, or abandoned and another one built.

The dwellings and the cleared fields were walled in by great stands of oak and walnut, and pine and beech. Now the rosy blossoms of the wild plum and the wild cherry brightened the woodlands, and along the forest floor the arbutus trailed its delicate pink flowers. The Pilgrims called it the mayflower after their ship. Wild strawberries were ripening, and the "birds sang in the woods most pleasantly."

As in so many other springs, the Indian women left their weaving of mats and baskets, and went out to the fields to plant corn when the unfolding leaves of the oak were "as big as a mouse's ear." Later they would also plant beans, squash, and pumpkins in the cornhills. They no longer hoed with the shell of the quahog, or hard-shell clam. Now they cultivated their corn with good English hoes that they had obtained by trading, and with which they could harvest bigger and better crops.

There was better fishing for the Indians, too, now that they used English fishhooks instead of the bent bones they once had to use. They came back with larger catches of shad and striped bass, with which the rivers teemed in the spring, and the iron kettles they got from the white man were much preferred by the Indian women to their old birchbark pots.

The Englishman's apparel appealed particularly to the men. They went almost naked in warm weather, but for protection in winter they came to value an English matchcoat more than the deerskin mantle they had been accustomed to wearing. Whatever odds and ends they could pick up were highly prized, too—a hat, a pair of stockings, shoes, a shirt, or a bright piece of cloth to tie around the waist.

The Wampanoag sachem himself had a special weakness for English goods, and was exceedingly fond of "elegant apparel." He still wore his ceremonial regalia—the beautiful fringed stole and the wampum accessories—but he was often seen in the English clothing he admired. Sometimes Philip appeared in odd combinations of the old and the new. An Englishman from abroad saw him walking proudly along a street in Boston one day dressed in a coat and buskins "thick-set with beads in pleasant wild works, and a broad belt of the same." The visitor estimated the value of his attire to be £20.

For trading purposes, the Wampanoags' stock of furs was meager. Their supply of wampum, or shell money, was limited, too, because they were not as adept in its production as the Narragansetts were. The one thing they had in abundance was land, and that was what the Englishmen wanted more than anything else.

Old Chief Massasoit had already given and sold large tracts of his hunting grounds to the English before his death in 1661. His seat had been at Sowams (now Warren, Rhode Island), a few miles to the north of Mount Hope, but his dominion had extended over nearly all of southeastern New England.

When Philip succeeded to the "throne" in 1662, he did not take stock of the diminishing Wampanoag lands. Instead, he sold off his territory to the English to satisfy his expensive taste for their merchandise. By 1671, he had waked up to the fact that his "kingdom" had shrunk to a very small domain. He now had no authority outside Mount Hope Peninsula and the eastern shore of Narragansett Bay. Philip had not been forced to sell his lands, but he felt bitter toward the English for having reduced his holdings to a few thousand acres. It was one of the grievances that were slowly building up to serious trouble.

It had not been like this during Massasoit's lifetime. He had been a loyal friend of the Plymouth settlers from the time of his first visit with them in 1622 until his death in 1661. Even toward the end of his life, when his counselors had warned of the growing power of the white men, he had remained faithful. Always he recalled the time when he had lain so close to death that his own medicine men had given up hope. His good friend Edward Winslow had hurried to Sowams

and had doctored him, and he had got well. In gratitude he had said, "Now I see the English are my friends
and love me, and while I live I will never forget this
kindness they have shown me."

Massasoit was survived by two sons, Wamsutta and
Metacom. It was not uncommon for the Indians to
take English names, and, as a mark of friendship, the
Plymouth authorities conferred the names of two ancient Greek kings upon the sons of the old chief. The
older became known as Alexander, and the younger
as Philip.

Alexander's reign was both brief and tragic. The
great leaders of Plymouth Colony who had been Massasoit's friends were dead. Younger men were in control now, and they were not so tactful or so considerate
in their relations with the Indians as their fathers had
been. Instead of friendliness and good will, there was
suspicion now.

Within the year of Alexander's succession, rumors
spread that he was conspiring with the Narragansetts
against Plymouth Colony, and he was summoned to
Duxbury for questioning. When he failed to come
promptly, he was escorted to the town by an armed
force that had been sent out to bring him in. But he
was soon dismissed by the authorities for lack of evidence against him. Before his return home, the young
sachem stopped at nearby Marshfield as the guest of
Josiah Winslow. Here he was suddenly taken ill with
a fever, and died soon after he was carried back to

Mount Hope. Word quickly passed around among the Wampanoags that the English had poisoned him.

Whatever the cause may have been, Philip firmly believed that the men of Plymouth were responsible for his brother's death. He began his reign, as Alexander's successor, with bitter feelings toward them. Their highhanded authority over his people rankled deeply. Before the white men came, the Wampanoags were a free and independent people. They had not been overpowered in battle by the English, but now they were treated like a subject race. Philip brooded upon the wrongs and injustices he felt had been inflicted upon him, and thought darkly of the future.

Halfway down, the hill of Mount Hope was cut across by a gray stone cliff. There was a natural stone bench near its base on which the sachem often sat when he conferred with his counselors. Here on his "throne" he saw his young warriors raise lean-muscled brown arms and heard them say: "We are strong. Lead us, great Chief, and we will cut down the white men as the North Wind flattens the weak reeds in our marshes."

Among the older warriors, Annawon was the one to whom Philip listened most attentively. Annawon had been his father's chief counselor. He was not one to make foolish boasts, but he too felt the time had come when his people must take a stand against the English if they were to survive as a proud race. Annawon spoke bitterly, not of the loss of their lands, but of the insults that hurt the Indian's pride and robbed him of his dignity.

Slowly puffing on his pipe, the old warrior talked about the injustices of the Plymouth court. "We are no longer a free people," he said. "Wherever we turn we break the white man's law, and are punished for it. They make bad Indians of our weak ones by selling them the white man's strong water, and then they say we are all bad."

Looking directly at Philip, Annawon continued: "And you, proud Chief, are treated like a bad Indian. They do to you what they did to your brother Alexander. You have no freedom; you must go to the Plymouth court to explain everything."

Even as the old counselor spoke, and soon after the Taunton interrogation, the court was busily bent upon making more trouble for the Wampanoag sachem. When the rest of his men failed to bring in their guns, the General Court convened at Plymouth in June and ordered "that all the guns that did belong to Philip now in our hands are justly forfeited," and ruled that they should be distributed among some of the Plymouth towns.

The court also commanded the sachem to come to Plymouth to explain why he had not kept his promises, but Philip indignantly refused to go. He also bluntly refused to give up any more firearms, insisting that he had agreed to part with only those guns that he and his men had left in Taunton. Alarmed by such contempt of authority, the General Court appointed a council of war, which issued warnings to all the colonies of the danger of Indian attack. And representatives were sent to the tribes along Cape Cod to try to extract promises of friendship and loyalty to the English.

The Massachusetts Government now attempted to arbitrate the dispute by first conferring with Philip. But Governor Prence and his assistants were infuriated when they learned that he had gone to Boston and had made complaints against Plymouth to Massachusetts Bay. They did not appreciate Governor John Leverett's mild rebuke, either. He had said in a letter that the Plymouth Government might be pushing Philip too hard, and suggested that commissioners from Massachusetts and Connecticut meet in Plymouth to review the case.

That the Wampanoag sachem had endeavored "to render the Government of Plymouth odious to Massachusetts" and that he had been up to his old trick of peddling "lies and false stories" about them the members of the council were sure, but they accepted Governor Leverett's suggestion.

Assured that the Bay Colony would be represented at the meeting, and again hopeful that he would be given fair treatment, Philip came with his chief men to Plymouth on September 24. Governor John Winthrop, Jr., of Connecticut and Governor Leverett of Massachusetts were there in the meetinghouse with the Plymouth governor and his assistants, and again the Wampanoag chieftain faced his accusers. The

Plymouth authorities spoke at great length about his insubordination—he had failed to bring in all of his firearms; he carried himself insolently and proudly, refusing to come to the Plymouth court when summoned; he had misrepresented matters to the Massachusetts magistrates.

Except that the hearings dragged on for five days, the conference was much like that at Taunton. Philip finally confessed that he had done wrong, and nothing more was said about the guns, but the sachem was warned by the council "to humble himself unto the Magistrates and to amend his ways if he expected peace; and that if he went on his refractory way, he must expect to smart for it."

Then there was the usual "treaty." Only, this time the terms were stiffer than ever before. Philip acknowledged that he was subject to the Government of Plymouth, and agreed to pay a fine of £100 within three years for the trouble he had caused, and to render an annual tribute of five wolves' heads in token of his loyalty. Moreover, he would consult only with the Plymouth Government about his differences; he would not make war without the governor's consent; and he would sell no more of his lands without the approval of the Plymouth court.

For the next three years there was peace between Plymouth Colony and the Wampanoags. Philip gave no outward sign of resentment toward the government that had forced him to bend the knee. He visited with white neighbors who were his friends. He called on his tailor in Boston. And, with Plymouth's permission, he continued to sell his lands to get the money he needed to dress in the English style.

With the help of a secretary, Philip carried on a correspondence with the English about business matters —such as, for example, this letter that was preserved in the records of the town of Dorchester, Massachusetts:

PHILIP, SACHEM OF MOUNT HOPE
TO CAPTAIN HOPESTILL FOSTER OF DORCHESTER
SENDETH GREETING:

Sir, you may please to remember that when I last saw you at Wading River, you promised me six pounds in goods. Now my request is that you would send by this Indian five yards of white or light colored serge to make me a coat; and a good Holland shirt ready made; and a pair of good Indian breeches, all of which I have present need of. Therefore I pray sir, fail not to send them by my Indian and with them the several prices of them; and silk and buttons and seven yards of trimming. Not else at present to trouble you with only the subscription of

KING PHILIP
HIS MAJESTY: P

MOUNT HOPE
the 15th of May, 1672

The Plymouth authorities relaxed. No rumors of rebellion agitated them. There was nothing, in fact, that now gave them cause to suspect Philip of wrongdoing. And early in 1674, the ban that had been in effect on the sale of firearms to the Indians was lifted.

3 Outbreak of War

Benjamin Church, who was born in Duxbury in 1639, was one of the most respected men in Plymouth Colony. His father, Richard Church, had designed the meetinghouse in Plymouth Town and had built the carriages for the guns that were mounted on top of Fort Hill. Needing more room for his growing family, he had moved to Duxbury across the harbor from Plymouth. Here the Church boys came to know the forest at their back door and the sea in front.

Young Benjamin hunted alone in the deep woods when he was almost too small to hold a musket. He was never afraid and he never got lost. He seemed to have been born with the instincts of a woodsman. In the fall and winter months, he used a shallop to hunt the waterfowl that flocked in great numbers to the salt marshes along the Duxbury shore. Long before he grew to the height of a man, he could sail a boat in all weathers on Cape Cod Bay.

The Plymouth lad often played with the Indian boys. He hunted and fished with them, too, and learned to shoot their bows and arrows. And he never forgot kind and friendly Chief Massasoit, who came now and again to Plymouth Town over the old Indian path that connected it with his own village of Sowams.

As a man grown tall and strong, Benjamin Church still had friends among the Indians. He knew more about them than most of the colonists, and was far more tolerant. He did not complain, as others did, about their filthiness, their laziness, and the habit many of them had of taking what did not belong to them. Church appreciated the good qualities he saw in the Indians, and believed they would in time become more civilized. "Why, look at what they've done with the Praying Indians," he was in the habit of saying when his English friends said: "You can't trust them. They are all liars and thieves."

Sometime in 1674, Benjamin Church moved his family down to the present town of Little Compton, Rhode Island. It was not far from the Sakonnet Indians on Sakonnet Point to the south, and was situated on a tract that had been sold to the English by Awashonks, their squaw sachem. Here Church made a good start by erecting two substantial houses, one of which he rented.

"If all goes well," he mused aloud, as he watched his barns going up and the fields made ready for planting, "I should have everything in good shape by spring. I think I shall like this new location."

"Are you sure there won't be trouble with the Indians, Mr. Church?" Charles Hazelton, his tenant's son, asked. "Philip, you know, lives not far from here. I've heard he can't control his wild young men. They want war."

"Look, my friend," Church replied, pointing northwestward across the Sakonnet River, "up yonder is Providence where Roger Williams lives. The Indians and he are good friends. Williams and I are good friends, too. Philip will not make war on his close neighbors. I believe he is too smart to start a war with anybody. He knows he couldn't win."

But in February of 1675, shocking news flashed through all the towns that jolted even Mr. Church's optimistic thinking. The body of John Sassamon, a well-known Praying Indian, was found under the ice of Assawompsett Pond a few miles south of Middleborough. And it was determined that he had been murdered.

Sassamon's parents were Christian converts, and he himself was a Praying Indian who had studied at

Harvard's Indian College, founded by the Reverend John Eliot, and had preached in the Praying Indian villages. Described as a "very cunning and plausible Indian, well skilled in the English language," he could both read and write English, and had assisted Eliot in translating the Bible in the Indian tongue.

For a time, John Sassamon acted as King Philip's secretary and interpreter. And he learned, to his horror, that the Wampanoag sachem was plotting to unite the other tribes in a war upon the English.

The unhappy Indian came to feel that he was being tossed about on the pitchforks of devils as conflicting loyalties clawed at his conscience. It was Christian, rather than Indian, loyalty that finally proved the stronger. He told Philip that he could not serve him any longer and that he wanted to return to his work in the Praying Indian villages. Sassamon did resume his preaching for a brief time after he had called on Governor Josiah Winslow of Plymouth Colony.

On the day when he appeared unannounced in Plymouth Town, John Sassamon went directly to Governor Winslow and, in private, unburdened himself with nervous haste. Refusing the chair the governor offered him, he stood twisting the brim of his black hat as he blurted out what he knew of Philip's secret plans. "The Chief is getting ready to make a big war on the white men," he said. "He tries to fool you. He says he is collecting guns to fight the Narragansetts. But Philip is trying to get the Narragansetts and other tribes to help him kill all the English."

"When will Philip go on the warpath against us?" Governor Winslow asked.

"In the spring of 1676," Sassamon replied. "He thinks he will have all the tribes on his side by then and that he will be ready." Looking fearfully around, he added: "It is a very great secret that I tell you. If Philip knows I have talked to you, he will kill me."

Governor Winslow was not convinced that the colonies were in peril, but he reported at once to the magistrates, in official secrecy, what Sassamon had told him. And the magistrates promptly conferred with the authorities in Boston.

The Reverend Increase Mather, distinguished pastor of Boston's North Church, and no friend of the Indians, was consulted. He expressed the opinion with which most of the colonists would have agreed when he scoffed, "This information has come from an Indian source, and we cannot believe the Indians even when they speak the truth."

Somehow, John Sassamon's "secret" leaked out. Just a week after his visit with Governor Winslow, several Indians happened to find his hat and gun lying beside a hole in frozen Assawompsett Pond, and recovered his body. Assuming that the Praying Indian had drowned accidentally, the men buried the corpse on the shore near the pond. The incident would have been closed if someone in Plymouth had not had second thoughts about how Sassamon might have met his death. His body was dug up, and upon closer examination it was found that he had been murdered; not only was the head badly bruised and swollen, but "his neck was broken by twisting of his head round, which is the way the Indians sometimes use when they practice murder."

Plymouth was not lax in law enforcement. The government was determined to track down and punish whoever was guilty of Sassamon's murder; there was good reason to suspect that it had been instigated by Philip. The information the authorities needed came from a friendly Indian by the name of Patuckson, who came voluntarily to see Governor Winslow. Like the unfortunate Sassamon, he had probably been wrestling with his conscience, for he had a grave report to make. He had seen John Sassamon murdered, he revealed, from a hilltop on which he stood unseen, and close enough to the pond that he could easily recognize the three Wampanoags who had committed the brutal crime, and had then tried to conceal it by pushing their victim's body under the ice to make it appear to have been an accidental drowning.

The alleged murderers were forthwith arrested— Tobias, one of Philip's counselors; Wampapaquan, son of Tobias; and Mattashunnamoo. Poor Sassamon's corpse was again taken out of the grave, and Increase Mather reported that "when Tobias came near the dead body it fell ableeding as fresh as if it had been newly slain, although it was buried a considerable time before that."

On the day of the trial the meetinghouse was crowded with people agog over one of the most sensational murders in the history of the colony. Before a jury of twelve Englishmen and six of the "most grave and sage Indians," the three defendants stoutly denied that they were guilty of murder as charged by the court. But with Patuckson on hand to testify against them, and to identify them as the men he had seen kill John Sassamon, the deliberations of the jurors were brief and the verdict was "Guilty." Since the Indian jurors had concurred in this opinion, the Plymouth Government was satisfied that justice had been done, and the murderers were sentenced to be hanged on June 8, 1675.

Tobias and Mattashunnamoo maintained their innocence to the very end, but after their execution Wampapaquan gave his story a different twist. Standing on the gallows, he declared that it was the other two Indians who had committed the murder and that he had stood by at Assawompsett Pond as an onlooker. His effort to save his own neck by placing the guilt upon the two dead Indians—it couldn't hurt them, he must have reasoned—earned him only a brief reprieve, for he was shot before the end of the month.

Excitement over the murder trial gave way to apprehensive speculation about the effect it would have on Philip. Just as no one doubted that he had decreed Sassamon's death, so no one doubted now that the sachem was seething with anger against the English for having interfered with Indian justice by trying and executing the three Wampanoags.

It was soon reported that Indian warriors from other

tribes had been seen coming into Mount Hope and that Philip had sent the Wampanoag women and children across the bay to take refuge with the Narragansetts. Settlers just across Taunton River told of having seen smoke rising from what appeared to be huge bonfires on Mount Hope Peninsula. They had heard the beating of drums, too, and a great noise that made them suspect that war dances were being held there.

About the same time an eerie report came from the sober inhabitants of Medfield, Massachusetts. They declared that on a Sunday morning they had heard the boom of a great gun from the south, followed by discharges of muskets. Others had cowered and run for shelter when "flying bullets" whizzed by just above their heads. Minutes later there was the ominous sound of the roll of drums. On that same day, people in several towns of Plymouth Colony had been startled by the noise of what seemed to be hard-riding troops galloping by. They had been heard but not seen, the frightened villagers said. And there were those who declared they had seen comets in the form of blazing arrows streaking across the black heavens.

The Plymouth authorities were not alarmed by the talk of flying bullets and invisible horsemen; in fact, they seemed not to have been aware of the gravity of the situation. Philip had appeared to be so amenable to discipline in the past that they believed he could be calmed down now by the friendly letter they sent him in which he was asked to dismiss his "foreign friends," and was assured that Plymouth "intended him no wrong nor hurt." The authorities had acted with un-accustomed restraint, but it was too late to try to win Philip over with assurances of good will. He made no reply to their message, and his warriors showed their defiance by shooting cattle of outlying settlers, stealing corn from them, and robbing their houses.

Some prominent Quakers of Rhode Island stepped in at this point and made an effort to avert what looked to them like impending war. On June 17, they conferred with Philip and some of his chief men on his own territory, and tried to persuade the sachem to agree to arbitration of his differences with Plymouth Colony, suggesting that the governor of New York act as one of the mediators. But Philip simply reiterated his grievances, and agreed to nothing.

The events of that spring of 1675 had troubled Ben-jamin Church so deeply that his hearty laugh was now seldom heard. When he was told the fantastic story about the invisible horsemen, he had smiled and said that perhaps they were the spirits of dead Indians racing through the towns to frighten the white men. But his thoughts had been of live Indians, not dead ones. He was not afraid of the spirits of the dead, but he had come to be haunted by the fear of what Philip and his young warriors might be doing up at Mount Hope.

Shortly after the Plymouth Government had sent word to Philip of its good intentions, two Indian run-ners came to see Church at his home in Little Compton. Sent by Awashonks, the squaw sachem of the Sakonnets, they told him that King Philip was preparing for war and that he had demanded that Awashonks make an alliance with him. She wanted Mr. Church's advice, and hoped that he would come to the dance that the Sakonnets would hold that night. Promising that he would be there, Church set out at once on horseback for the appointed place.

Awashonks and her subjects were in the midst of the tribal dance when he arrived early in the evening. Streaked and smeared with paint, the dark bodies of the warriors shone in the firelight as the squaw sachem led them in the contortions of the wild dance. She, too, was heavily painted, and ropes of beads hanging from her neck bounced as she whirled in rhythm to the drumbeats.

The dance ended abruptly as Church walked into the circle of firelight. Wiping the sweat from her face, Awashonks sat down and beckoned him to take a seat beside her. After an exchange of formal greetings, the squaw sachem said: "Two of my men have come back from King Philip's war dance, and he has sent six of his Wampanoags to draw me into an alliance against the English. Tell me, Mr. Church, is it true that the men of Plymouth are getting ready to invade Philip's country? These Wampanoags here say that is so."

Church shook his head vigorously and assured Awashonks that he had been in Plymouth only a few days before and knew that Governor Winslow was not preparing for war. Troops, he said, were out trying to catch bad Indians who had broken the law. It was nothing more than that. Then he added, "Do you think that I would have bought land here and built a new home if I had thought there was danger of war between King Philip and the English?"

Awashonks seemed to be impressed by this. She now commanded the Wampanoags to come forward, and they pushed their way through the crowd. Garishly painted, and with their slick black hair trimmed and dressed up high like a cockscomb, they ignored Church and faced Awashonks. Church observed that they carried powder horns and bullet pouches on their backs, and knew that this meant they were preparing for war.

When Awashonks repeated what Church had told her, the Mount Hope warriors darted angry glances at him, and snarled, "He lies."

Church stepped over to the tallest of the insolent braves and, feeling his bullet-filled pouch, asked, "What for?"

The young Indian sneeringly answered, "To shoot pigeons."

Turning to Awashonks, Benjamin Church said, "If Philip wants war, knock down these upstarts and then hurry to the English for protection."

The six Wampanoags glared but said nothing. Little Eyes, one of Awashonks' counselors, requested that Church have a private talk with him. Whereupon the other chief men protested angrily, and loud mutterings arose among the Sakonnets. Trouble was barely averted when Church heatedly told the Wampanoags that they were wild dogs that thirsted for the blood of their English neighbors, who had never done them any wrong but instead had shown them kindness. "Go back," he said, "and tell King Philip I think he is an old man whose eyes are dim. He cannot see that the English will destroy him if he makes war. He is too weak to rebel against the thousands of Englishmen who will burn his wigwams, trample down his cornfields, and kill off his warriors."

Benjamin Church had always befriended the Indians, but he was appalled by the terrible prospect of war. He turned angrily against Philip and his hostile braves because he knew what the cost of such a conflict would be, both to the Indians and to the white settlers.

He said to Awashonks as he started to leave: "Stay away from Philip. Go to Plymouth. If you join Philip and his madmen in a rebellion against the English, it will mean your death. The Sakonnets will be crushed. I will go to Governor Winslow and make arrangements for your protection." Awashonks thanked him, and ordered two of her men to accompany him back to Little Compton.

Early the next morning Church mounted his horse again and departed for a visit with Weetamoo. The squaw sachem of the Pocassets was the sister of Philip's wife. She had been married to his brother Alexander, and was now the wife of an Indian named Peter Nunnuit. As King Philip's sister-in-law, she too might have news that Governor Winslow should know. Moreover, Weetamoo had long been a friend of Church's family, and he was concerned for her safety.

Near the main village of the Pocassets, Benjamin Church met Peter Nunnuit. He had just returned from a war dance at Mount Hope, and was bursting with news of all that he had seen and heard.

"There will be war, Mr. Church," he said. "Young warriors from many parts are there in Philip's country. Annawon has orders to attack if the English start the shooting." As they walked up the hill toward the squaw sachem's lodge, Peter Nunnuit spoke fearfully of the hatred that Philip's warriors had shown toward the colonists. "Fight the English! Kill the English— *now!*" they had yelled. Peter further informed Mr. Church that Philip had promised to let them go plundering at the rising of the new moon. "But they will make the English draw the first blood," he said, referring to the superstition that the side that did that would lose.

Weetamoo was glad to see her old friend. She shook her head with grave concern as she told him that most of her warriors had gone to Philip's dance and had not yet returned. "Philip is being forced into war by his young men," she said regretfully. "If he does not let them have their way, someone else may become chief."

"You must not follow Philip," Church warned her. "He is not strong enough to win a war with the English. Go to Plymouth. I shall see the governor soon, and I will urge him to protect all the friendly Indians."

Weetamoo answered Church with a worried look. "I do not know, Mr. Church," she said. "My sister wants me to be with her."

It was Peter Nunnuit who gave Church a final warning. "Do not travel the main trails," he said. "Ride by night. The Wampanoags will not attack while the spirits of their dead are haunting the forest at night. Be on your guard, Mr. Church."

Worried and depressed, Benjamin Church rode off through the dark woods. In Plymouth Town a few days later, he heard the news that left every man, woman, and child in all the colonies stricken with terror. Swansea had been attacked by Philip's warriors.

Unlike most of the towns in Plymouth Colony, Swansea was not closely built up around a village green. The main settlement of scattered houses was situated just across the Kickamuit River at the entrance to Mount Hope Peninsula. Some distance to the south, eighteen houses stood within the narrow neck leading to Philip's domain, and farther down, to the southeast, other outlying settlers had built their houses at Mattapoiset. Relations between the English and the Wampanoags had been friendly, and even after the execution of Sassamon's murderers the people of Swansea could not believe that serious trouble was brewing. Philip would surely curb his wild young warriors, they reassured one another.

But when the Indians began looting some of the houses on the neck of land that joined Mount Hope to the mainland, many of the settlers in that area took fright, and hastily sought refuge in the main part of the settlement of Swansea. And the rest of the terrified people followed in a general exodus after two of the deserted houses were burned down by bands of marauding Indians.

On Sunday, June 20, while most of the inhabitants of Swansea were attending services at the meetinghouse, several young Wampanoags came swaggering along the road. At the first house they entered, they encountered the owner and demanded permission to grind their hatchets. When it was refused, because, the man said, it was the Lord's day, on which no unnecessary work should be done, one of the Indians insolently replied, "We care neither for your God nor for you, and we will grind our hatchets." Having done so, they ransacked the house, took what they wanted, and helped themselves to food.

Farther down the road, they chanced upon another settler. They forced him to go with them, taunting and ridiculing him as they jostled him along. Finally they let him go with the sneering remarks: "Now be a good man. Tell no lies and do no work on the Lord's day."

After shooting some cattle in the pastures nearby, the Wampanoags entered the narrow neck on their way back to Mount Hope. In a deserted house they came unexpectedly upon the owner and his son, who had returned to look after their property. The young boy promptly raised his musket and mortally wounded one of the Indians. With hideous yells, the other Wampanoags lifted their fallen comrade and quickly carried him off down the road. According to tradition, Philip had been told by his medicine men that he could win only if the English drew the first blood; and now his warriors had provoked the enemy into doing this as an auspicious beginning for the Indians in a war with the English.

The colonists no longer doubted that the Wampanoag sachem intended to loose the pent-up fury of the Indians upon them. After the plundering of the houses on the neck began, the people of Swansea had rushed word of their critical situation to Governor Winslow. The Plymouth governor at once sent an urgent message to Boston, informing Governor Leverett of the alarming developments and asking for help. The response from Massachusetts was prompt. A few days after Plymouth troops had taken the old Indian trail that passed through Middleborough, Bridgewater, and Taunton, troopers and foot soldiers from the Bay Colony were marching southward to Swansea by way of Dedham and Rehoboth.

In the meantime, Benjamin Church had seen Governor Winslow and had asked him to protect Awashonks and Weetamoo. But the governor shook his head. "I can give no assurance for their safety, Mr. Church," he said brusquely. "There is too much bitterness against the Indians."

"But Awashonks and Weetamoo are not hostile," Church argued. "They—"

The governor cut him off, saying emphatically, "We can't take the risk." Church dropped the subject and agreed to go with the Plymouth forces to Swansea.

The first contingent, under the command of Captain William Bradford (son of the earlier Governor Bradford), reached Swansea late in the day of the twenty-first. They were posted at the several garrison houses into which the people had crowded for safety. The fortified house of the Reverend John Miles stood near the bridge that spanned the Kickamuit River and led into Wampanoag territory. Some distance from it was the Browne garrison, and at Mattapoiset the settlers had found refuge in the Bourne house.

Thursday, the twenty-fourth of June, had been designated by the Plymouth Government as a day of humiliation and prayer—a day on which the terrified people would entreat the Lord "to go forth with our forces and bless, succeed, and prosper them; delivering them from the hands of His enemies, and returning them all safely to their families and relations again."

It was the day, too, when bands of Wampanoag warriors stole silently into Swansea with the intent to kill, and concealed themselves behind bushes and trees along the roads and paths. Among the first victims of the ambush were people returning from services at the meetinghouse. A blast of gunfire from a roadside thicket killed one man and wounded several others. A settler who had sent his wife and child ahead while he attempted to snatch up a few belongings was shot dead on the threshold of his front door. Hearing the shot, his wife turned back and tried to reach her husband, but within seconds she and her young son were murdered and scalped.

Two men left the Miles garrison house to draw water from the well. On the way they toppled over, pierced by bullets. The Indians ran from cover, seized the quivering bodies, and dragged them into the woods. They were found later, scalped and with hands and feet cut off. At Mattapoiset a party of men left the garrison to recover some corn at a deserted farm, and eight of them never returned—they, too, fell riddled with bullets.

After nightfall the emboldened Wampanoags crept close to the Miles garrison, strongest of the fortified houses, and shot one sentry dead and wounded two others. Before they returned to Mount Hope Peninsula, the Indians also shot and killed the two men who made a dash for Rehoboth to fetch a doctor to treat the wounded.

King Philip's War had begun. That the Wampanoag sachem had been getting ready for it by trying to organize the other tribes in a conspiracy to wipe out Plymouth Colony seems certain. But the outbreak of hostilities caught him unprepared, for he had not yet succeeded in cementing the alliance. His hot-blooded young warriors had been clamoring for war before Sassamon's betrayal of their chief, and Philip was not strong enough to restrain them after Plymouth exe-

cuted the Wampanoag murderers. Instead of waiting
for a well-organized attack that could have been sudden, widespread, and devastating, the impatient young
braves had come out of their lair and engaged in plundering and random killings that gave both Plymouth
and Massachusetts warning and time to mobilize the
forces that were rushed to Swansea.

Philip had been stung with resentment by the in-
dignities he had suffered at the hands of the tactless
and overbearing leaders of Plymouth Colony, and for
a long time he had been obsessed by his grievances. He
could not forget that Massasoit, his father, had been
a great chief who had befriended the English when
they were weak in numbers and in resources, and had
helped them to become strong.

He could not forget, either, that the old sachem had
once ruled a domain as wide as all of southeastern New
England and that now he, Philip, his son, was hemmed
in on one small peninsula. But Philip did not blame
himself for having recklessly sold off much of his land
to satisfy his weakness for English goods. It was cause
only for a deepening resentment when he saw his
former territory increase in value after it was occupied
and improved by the white men. At every turn, Philip
felt tricked, trapped, insulted, and mistreated by them,
and his anger smoldered dangerously until it finally
flared up in the flames of war.

There was no reason the outbreak of war should
have been the shock it was to the English. They had

received warnings of Philip's hostile intentions not only from Sassamon before he met his death at Assawompsett Pond but also from Waban, a native preacher at Natick. The Wampanoags intended "mischief," he had reported in the spring of 1675, and were only waiting for the trees to leaf out that they might better conceal themselves.

And the colonists were as bewildered by Philip's having turned against them as they were shocked. Soon after the attack on Swansea, Governor Winslow wrote: "I do solemnly protest that we know not anything which might have put Philip upon these notions, nor have we heard that he pretends to have suffered any wrong from us, save only that we had killed [executed] some Indians."

It was a strange admission for the governor of Plymouth Colony to make after years of humiliating and harassing the Wampanoag sachem. The authorities had tried to be fair and just to the natives, but it was justice by the white man's standards, the inevitable dominance over the weaker by the stronger race.

Failing to see that the war had been brought about by themselves, the Puritans looked upon it as sent by God. And why was the Deity punishing them? How had they erred so grievously that they were being afflicted with the horrors of savage warfare? The clergy believed it was "retribution for sins of the younger generation who fidgeted under hour-long sermons, let their hair grow, wore fashionable clothes, and drank rum." The Massachusetts General Court gave as another reason the colony's laxity in persecuting the Quakers. And the Rhode Island Friends let it be known that they believed war had come because the Bay Colony had treated the Quakers so harshly.

4 The Battle of the Peas Field

The war had come before Philip was ready for it, but, with the assistance of other tribes, the Indians would not lack advantages. New England was still heavily wooded country, sparsely settled, and traversed by rough trails. It was ideal terrain for the Indians. They knew the trackless swamps, the tortuous paths, the forest fastnesses, and the fording places of the rivers. They could move silently and swiftly through the woods unencumbered by heavy clothing and equipment, lie patiently in ambuscades, strike quickly, and as rapidly draw off. Moreover, they knew a good deal about the settlers—knew where and how they lived; and they had become expert in the use of the white man's firearms.

The English were not well prepared for war, and knew nothing about forest warfare, which was the kind of fighting they would have to do with the Indians. Nearly all able-bodied men had been required to serve in the militia, and for training they had drilled on the village greens several times a year. Every man had to furnish his own equipment—a flintlock musket, a sword or cutlass, a knapsack, and, slung over the left shoulder, a broad belt or bandolier with loops and pockets for carrying a supply of powder and bullets.

By June 28, 1675, Captain Bradford's troops in Swansea had been reinforced by a second Plymouth company of foot soldiers under seventy-seven-year-old Captain James Cudworth; by a troop of Bay cavalrymen under Captain Daniel Henchman, and another under Captain Thomas Prentice; and by a volunteer company of foot soldiers from Boston commanded by Captain Samuel Moseley. Described as an "excellent soldier and an undaunted spirit," Moseley was a tough adventurer whose company was composed of seamen, apprentices, and servants, and a few pirates he had captured in the West Indies who had been released from jail to fight Indians.

Protection was given the Browne and Bourne garrisons, and the officers set up their headquarters in the Miles house. Soldiers camped around it within the shelter of a barricade they had erected.

In the absence of Major Thomas Savage, the commanding officer who had not yet arrived from Massachusetts, Plymouth's Captain Cudworth gave reluctant permission to a small company of Bay horsemen to go out and explore the Indian territory beyond the bridge. Their enthusiasm for engaging the enemy that day was soon quenched by an attack from ambush that cost the life of one man and the wounding of another. Benjamin Church, who had come along too, was dismayed to see the rest of the troopers wheel about and go galloping back to the safety of the barricade. He was even more disgusted when it became evident that no reinforcements were coming from the garrison. "The Lord have mercy on us," he shouted at the retreating horsemen as he followed in the rear, "if a handful of Indians shall thus dare such an army!"

Early in the evening of the twenty-ninth, Major Savage rode into Swansea with two small units of cavalry, bringing the total number of men to 500. He gave orders at once for a full-scale invasion of Mount Hope Peninsula on the following day.

A dismal rain was falling the next morning, and it was not until around noon that the various companies were ready to march. The day became all the drearier after the troops crossed the bridge and passed the charred ruins of the outlying settlers' homes that had been fired by the Indians. A few miles farther on, the advancing columns reached the narrowest part of the neck, and here they stopped to look upon a chilling sight. Stuck up on poles were the severed heads of the eight Englishmen who had been killed at Mattapoiset on June 24. Church remarked that these "gashed and ghostly objects struck a damper on all beholders."

After the remains of the victims had been taken down and buried, the troops moved on into the green, leafy peninsula, on the alert for the Wampanoags they expected to find. But the farther they ranged, the less vigilant they became, for it was soon evident that they were in deserted territory. The wigwams were there, many of them, but all were empty. Soldiers poked around Philip's lodge on Mount Hope, and found no one. It was the telltale absence of canoes along the shore that finally made it clear to the English that Philip and his warriors had escaped across Narragan-sett Bay to take refuge in the Pocasset country to the southeast.

Upon their return to Swansea, Major Savage debated with his officers what they should do next, and decided to build a fort on the eastern side of the peninsula near the mouth of the Kickamuit River. "We should have a fort here to hold the first ground we have won," the major said.

Benjamin Church sputtered. "Yes, ground won by the Indians leaving it to us—a fine victory! Come," he urged, "let's set out in hot pursuit of Philip over on the Pocasset side where he has probably gone to enlist Weetamoo's Indians. What would be the good of a small fort here anyway? How could we defend it surrounded by red demons?"

But Church's sound advice was ignored, and the army lost the opportunity to thwart Philip's designs and bring the war to a quick end. This might have been accomplished if a strong force had been sent at once into the Pocasset country to corner Philip, as Church had suggested, while the rest of the army took up a position around Taunton to cut off the Indians who tried to escape to the northwest.

While the officers at Swansea hesitated, fumbled, and wasted precious time, the authorities in Boston had been thinking uneasily about the powerful Narragansetts, recalling the old rumors that Philip had been trying to draw them into his conspiracy and had sent the Wampanoag women and children into their country for safety. The outcome was a decision by the Council of War to send a military mission to try to extract from their sachems a treaty favorable to the English.

The negotiations were not entrusted to a handful of peace commissioners. Instead, orders were carried to Swansea by Captain Edward Hutchinson that detached most of the Massachusetts troops there for the undertaking. On July 5, the army started out for the conference with impressive strength, "to make peace with a sword" if necessary.

Somewhere in the depths of the Narragansett country, the important sachems must have laughed at the efforts of the English to force them to make peace, for they did not even come to Wickford, Rhode Island, where the negotiations were conducted. They sent four of their men to represent them as "counselors." These representatives balked so frequently at the demands of the English that the negotiations dragged on for many days. Finally, on July 15, an agreement was reached by which the Narragansetts promised many things—mainly, that they would treat the Wampanoags as enemies and would hand over to the English any of Philip's men who should fall into their hands.

The Narragansett chiefs probably laughed again when they were given a report on the negotiations, for they had no intention of abiding by the terms of the agreement, which they had not approved in the first place.

While the Massachusetts peace negotiators were conferring with the Narragansetts at Wickford, the Plymouth troops in Swansea marked time until the aged Captain Cudworth decided that more supplies were needed, and hiked off to Plymouth with a large part of his force. His stay was short, for the day after his arrival the authorities ordered him back to Swansea. And now, during the absence of the Bay troops, Captain Matthew Fuller was ordered to take about forty men into the Pocasset country to talk peace with Weetamoo. Having "grown ancient and heavy," Fuller feared the hardships of the undertaking would be too great for him, but he would be assisted by Benjamin Church, who preferred any assignment to working on the fort that was being erected on Mount Hope Peninsula.

After having been ferried over to Aquidneck Island and from there to the Pocasset shore, the small force was divided into two groups. Captain Fuller marched off with half of the men, and Church went in another direction with the rest. When Fuller and his group descried some Indians in the distance, they quickly hid in an abandoned house near the water. Since the heavy old captain was not bearing up well, he was more than willing to be rescued by a boat that came along and carried him and his men back to Aquidneck Island.

Church and his little party were nosing through the woods like a pack of hunting dogs. Presently the men complained that they hadn't seen any sign of the Indians their leader had told them they would find in the Pocasset woods. "There will be Indians soon now —and enough," Church assured them, pointing to freshly made tracks they had just come upon. He was certain they would lead to an Indian encampment.

Following the trail, they came in sight of a field where two Indians were gathering peas. Church called to them, but instead of answering or coming forward, they dashed into the underbrush of woods close to the peas field on one side. Church's little company raced in pursuit. Just before they reached the field, the Indians fired a volley that sent bullets whistling around them, but no one was hit.

Church quickly dispersed his men. Some were ordered "to clap under the fence and lie close," and the rest to move cautiously into the field and to be ready to fire if the enemy appeared. Then Benjamin Church looked up and saw the appalling sight of a hill "that seemed to move, being covered with Indians, with their bright guns glittering in the sun."

There was just one chance of escape—to retreat to the shore nearby. Church prayed that a boat would come to their rescue before they were overpowered by the Indians. They outnumbered his men fifteen to one, and could easily have overwhelmed the English by a concerted rush. Instead, they chose to advance warily, intending to pick the Englishmen off one by one, without any loss to themselves.

Church knew how to make use of every means of shelter as well as the Indians did, but the advantages were all on their side. They had come out of ambush on the hillside, and were now crouched behind "every rock, stump, tree, and fence in sight," yelling like devils, and shrieking vengeance.

But the Englishmen, who hugged the ground behind a low embankment, ducked the bullets, and answered the incessant fire with an accuracy of marksmanship that now and again brought down an Indian who tried to leap from stump to tree. Church stayed close to his soldiers, directing their maneuvers and firing upon the enemy at the same time.

Hard pressed as they were, it looked as if the men were being slowly pushed into the Sakonnet River. Church himself was cautiously moving backward toward the shore, prayerfully hoping that a vessel would soon come. If no help came, he intended to make a desperate stand and fight until the last bullet was spent, and he and the last of his men were killed. It would be better to die fighting than to fall into hands that usually scalped and tortured before they killed.

The Englishmen were upon stony ground. The only protection they had now was the breastwork of stones they had hastily thrown up. Church had ordered them to take off their coats so that the Rhode Islanders on the opposite shore would see their white shirts and would know they were Englishmen in peril. Just when their ammunition was almost used up, a boat did come over. But the Indians saw it, too, and "plied their shot so warmly" that the crew refused to send a canoe through the shallow water to rescue the men who were shouting for help. One of the men cried out in despair, "For heaven's sake, take us off—our ammunition is almost gone!"

But those aboard the vessel callously turned about and sailed away, leaving the soldiers to what looked like certain death. The Indians could see what had happened. They quickened their fire and whooped their satisfaction.

Now there was talk among the exhausted Englishmen of taking to their heels. Church argued and pleaded. Escape by flight was impossible, he pointed out. If they would continue to be patient, courageous, and prudently sparing of the ammunition they had left, a boat would surely come soon and rescue them.

Then, observing one of his men exposed for a moment, he yelled, "Up with that stone, man—quick!" Seconds later a bullet struck the upended flat stone with a whacking thud as the soldier held it like a shield before him.

Hope, as well as ammunition and daylight, was almost gone when a sloop was sighted moving down the river from the north. It was another boatload of cowards, the soldiers suspected. But as the vessel drew nearer, Church thought he recognized the skipper as Captain Roger Goulding. "If it is Goulding," he said to his men, "he'll fetch us out of this hell-hole, for he is just the man for this kind of risky business."

It *was* Captain Goulding, and, as Church said, he was the man to effect a rescue in the face of danger. With enemy bullets spitting into his sails, he quickly followed the directions Church shouted to him. A small canoe, made fast to a rope on the sloop, was lowered, and a fresh wind drove it ashore. Only two men could be transported at a time. Covered by gunfire from the sloop and from the Englishmen on the shore, all the men were rescued. Benjamin Church was the last to leave, and as a final gesture of contempt for his foes, he fired one last shot at them.

That was the end of the skirmish that had begun in the peas field of Captain John Almy. For about five hours the little band of twenty men had successfully defended themselves against a company of shrieking Indians who greatly outnumbered them. They had not been stricken with panic by the savage yells and the perilous assault, and they could now pride themselves on being seasoned Indian fighters. And, even though a peace parley with the Pocassets had failed to materialize, Benjamin Church had proved his prowess and his courage as a leader in the encounter with the Indians.

In the meantime, the enemy had attacked several other Plymouth towns. In the small settlement of Middleborough most of the houses were burned down, but the inhabitants were lucky. Warned in time, they escaped by fleeing to nearby Plymouth Town. At Dartmouth, in the extreme southern part of the colony, thirty dwellings were destroyed, and a number of the people were slain. And out on the Massachusetts frontier a band of Nipmucks suddenly appeared at the little settlement of Mendon and killed several colonists.

When Benjamin Church got back to Mount Hope —to what he called "the losing fort"—he found that Major Savage had returned from what would prove to have been a futile expedition into the Narragansett country. The major now decided that it would be a good plan after all to follow the advice Church had given him before the fort was built. The English would at last pursue Philip into the Pocasset Swamp where Church believed he had probably holed up. Before the army went into action, however, Major Savage wanted more information about the enemy's headquarters. The man who had already seen action in the Battle of the Peas Field was the scout who readily undertook the assignment.

At the outset, Church had the good fortune to meet an Indian, known as John Alderman, on Aquidneck Island. Alderman and his family were now refugees from the Pocassets, deserters who had fled from Squaw Sachem Weetamoo's camp. The Indian willingly gave Church much valuable information, and a few days later he was on his way with a detachment of soldiers to the Pocasset country to obtain the firsthand facts the army wanted.

After several brushes with the enemy, Church and his company arrived safely at the edge of a dense cedar swamp. Most likely it was here that Philip lay concealed. Smoke from the enemy's fires could be seen, and Church's force penetrated the swamp far enough to hear the high-pitched babble of Indian voices. This must certainly be King Philip's hide-out, Church concluded. He turned back to carry the intelligence to Major Savage as speedily as possible.

Acting upon the information brought by Benjamin Church, the army left Swansea and arrived in Taunton on the evening of July 17. The next day the troops marched south to the swamp near the eastern shore of Narragansett Bay, where they hoped to capture King Philip.

5 Ordeal at Brookfield

Late in the afternoon of July 19, the main force of several hundred soldiers arrived at Pocasset Swamp. The light was almost gone from the cedar thickets, where tangled undergrowth made penetration difficult. But Major Savage decided to enter the swamp without delay. At first the men proceeded with caution, trampling down the brush and bending back the tangle of vines and branches as noiselessly as possible.

The dark forms that they presently glimpsed slithering snakelike through the thickets in the gloom were there for a purpose—to lure the English deeper into the swamp.

The men fell unsuspectingly into the trap. Forgetting prudence at sight of the Indians, they pressed on and came at length to a small clearing. Free to move faster, they had quickened their pace when suddenly a volley of shots spurted out of the dark woods. Several soldiers dropped dead; others were wounded.

After this sudden burst of gunfire, there was silence in the swamp. The invisible enemy seemed to have vanished, and the bewildered troops fumbled about, not knowing what they should do. Fearful of another attack, they had their muskets primed and ready to shoot. But they soon realized that, with night coming on, they could not be certain whether they were taking aim at a bush, an Indian, or one of their own men. In this predicament, Major Savage ordered a retreat. So the troops wearily turned back, stumbling along, tripping over roots and each other, falling and painfully scratching their hands and faces on thorny vines that they could not see in the dark. They knew now how dangerous it was "to fight in such dismal woods, when their eyes were muffled with the leaves, and their arms pinioned with the thick boughs of the trees, and with their feet continually shackled by the roots spreading every way in those boggy woods."

In camp the next morning, the officers were more cheerful and more hopeful. They unanimously decided that they did not like "fighting a wild beast in his own den" and that it was not necessary to do so. Why go into the lair of the lion when the entrance could be blocked and the beast starved into submission? It seemed as simple and as logical as that.

Therefore, it was concluded that, with Philip penned up in the swamp as securely as if they had him in an iron-barred cage, such a large force was not needed to guard him. The decision to withdraw and disperse most of their superior forces at this critical point was the worst blunder the English had made. The aged and bumbling Captain Cudworth marched back with the Plymouth troops to Swansea and the fort on Mount Hope Peninsula. Prentice and his troops rode out to reconnoiter in the country around Mendon, and Major Savage returned to Boston with the bulk of the Bay forces. Captain Daniel Henchman was left with something over a hundred soldiers and a few friendly Indians to police the swamp, and to build a fort on the southwestern side between the swamp and the bay.

Apparently it did not occur to the commanding officers that they might have caught their quarry if they had made a vigorous assault upon the swamp in broad daylight. When Benjamin Church left the Pocasset country, he was breathing fire over all the bungling. He went back to his family in Little Compton to attend to his personal affairs. For four months, from August through November, 1675, he took no part in the war.

It happened that building was going on simultaneously inside and outside the swamp after the departure of most of the English troops. Deep within the interior, Philip's husky braves were busy cutting down cedar trees and building rafts. Outside the swamp, English sentinels paced their beats while the rest of the men labored at constructing the fort.

Sometime during the evening of July 30, Lieutenant Nathaniel Thomas and James Brown appeared unexpectedly at Henchman's camp. They had come in great haste from Rehoboth to report the alarming news they had heard there—King Philip had escaped! It had not been a difficult feat for the Wampanoag sachem. With full knowledge of the scanty force that had been left to guard him, he had seized the opportunity to flee with his warriors through the unguarded north end of the swamp. Somewhere along the eastern bank of the Taunton River they had crossed over to the opposite shore on the rafts and in the canoes they had brought along. And Squaw Sachem Weetamoo and her people had gone with them.

Captain Henchman did not take up pursuit of the Wampanoags, fleeing northwestward toward the Nipmuck country, until daybreak of the thirty-first, when he moved his troops across the river by boat and marched on to Providence. The next day he joined forces with some Rehoboth men and friendly Mohegan warriors who were already on the heels of the Wampanoags. But when the combined forces finally overtook them, it was too late. After a short, sharp encounter, the Indians eluded their pursuers by taking refuge in a swamp. Henchman gave up the chase, and Weetamoo and her people escaped to the Narragan-setts, and Philip and his warriors went on up the Blackstone Valley to join the Nipmucks.

These Indians were more numerous than the Wam-panoags, but, like the Narragansetts, they were not so well organized. They lived in scattered villages, and each separate group was under an independent sachem or sagamore, the most powerful of whom were Monoco, or One-Eyed John, Matoonas, Shoshanim, or Sagamore Sam, and Muttaump.

Having a number of isolated settlements in the Nip-muck country, Massachusetts Bay was anxious to have pledges of friendship from this tribe. Instead of send-ing an army this time to negotiate with the sachems, the authorities accepted the offer of a remarkably brave and resourceful young trader to talk with them in the interests of peace. Ephraim Curtis knew the Nipmucks well, for he owned a trading post in their country. He set out on the dangerous mission from Marlborough the second week in July, accompanied by two other white men and a few friendly Indians.

After a tortuous journey deep into Nipmuck terri-tory, Curtis delivered his message of peace to a hostile gathering of sachems, and then departed. He learned upon his return to Boston that it was Matoonas who had led the attack on Mendon in which several people were murdered. Undaunted, Ephraim Curtis made one more hazardous visit to the Nipmucks later in

July. After making another plea for peace in behalf of Governor John Leverett, he was promised that two sachems would call on the governor in the near future —but it proved to be an empty gesture.

From the beginning of hostilities the Praying Indians had not only been loyal to the English but had shown a willingness to fight on their side. In spite of the distrust many of the colonists felt toward these Christian Indians, both Plymouth and Massachusetts had accepted their services. Early in the war, too, Uncas, sachem of the Mohegans in eastern Connecticut, had avowed his intention of giving aid to the English. Since then, some of his warriors had joined the white troops in their efforts to capture Philip.

When, toward the end of July, none of the Nipmuck sachems had come to Boston to discuss peace as they had promised to do, the authorities decided to take a firmer stand by sending an armed force to parley with them. They also intended to demand that the Indians who had committed the murders at Mendon be handed over to the English for punishment. This assignment, fraught with perilous uncertainty, was given to Captain Edward Hutchinson, and Captain Thomas Wheeler was ordered to accompany him with twenty-odd troopers. Ephraim Curtis and three friendly Indians, who went along as guides and interpreters, were also in the party that left Cambridge on July 28, took the old Bay Path, and rode on through Sudbury and out into the Nipmuck wilderness. They passed through a number of villages in which the wigwams stood empty and the cornfields deserted. Obviously, and ominously, the Indians had departed to gather in some central location.

Far out in the forested country of the Nipmucks, the mounted Englishmen came to the tiny settlement of Brookfield. About twenty families lived here in lonely isolation, but without fear of their Indian neighbors, for there had been no friction between them. Upon learning that most of the Nipmucks were assembled ten miles to the northwest of the village, Captain Hutchinson sent Curtis with a small group of men on August 1 to make contact with the Indians, and to inform them that the English troopers had not come to harm them but to deliver a message. Curtis was not received with friendliness, but some of the sachems agreed to a rendezvous with Hutchinson on the following morning at eight o'clock, the place of meeting to be under a large tree three miles from Brookfield.

The entire party, accompanied by three settlers, rode off briskly early the next day, and shortly drew rein in the shade of the big tree. No Indians were there to meet them, and as time passed it became increasingly evident that the sachems did not intend to keep their promise to come for the parley. The three Indian scouts suspected treachery, and urged the officers to turn back, but the Brookfield settlers persuaded them that it would be safe to go on. So Hutchinson and Wheeler decided to ride on for some distance with the foolish idea that the Nipmucks might have misunderstood the directions and would be waiting for them in the wooded area farther north. The captains were right in their surmise that these "friendly" Indians were waiting for them there.

The horsemen came at length to a narrow pass. A rocky, wooded hill rose steeply on the right, and a swamp covered with brush and tall grass spread out on the left. Benjamin Church would never have ventured through a defile in such circumstances. But there was no sign of danger on that warm, sunny August day. The only sound was the muffled clopping of the horses' hoofs on the dusty trail as the riders entered the narrow path and started through, one behind the other in single file.

When they had gone halfway, the silence seemed suddenly to explode. A terrific detonation erupted from an ambuscade on the right as the Indians fired simultaneously on the little force trapped in the pass. Eight men, including the three Brookfield settlers, dropped dead from their saddles and were trampled by the flying hoofs of the frightened horses. Charging down from their hiding place, the Indians closed in upon the rest of the horsemen, cutting off their escape in front and in the rear. Captain Wheeler's mount was shot from under him, and as he fell he was struck by a bullet. His son had been hit, too, but in the confusion he was able to help his father into the saddle of a riderless horse. Captain Hutchinson, who had been seriously wounded, was also saved from falling into the hands of the Indians by the survivors, who finally fought their way up the steep hillside, having left the dead behind.

They would in all likelihood have been overtaken along the main path and wiped out by the Nipmucks if the two remaining Indian scouts had not known of a circuitous trail by which they led the hard-riding English survivors back to Brookfield. The third friendly Indian had been captured.

The exhausted troopers—the bloody remnant of the gallant company that had ridden off that morning to talk peace—quickly alerted the inhabitants to the peril of an Indian attack. The largest and strongest house in the settlement was that of Sergeant John Ayres, and the terrified people rushed in frantic haste to this shelter, bringing with them such provisions and supplies as they had hurriedly snatched up. The men had brought their muskets and ammunition, and now about eighty people, most of them women and children, crouched together in the garrison house, fearfully awaiting the expected assault.

Their situation was critical. The defenders knew they could not hold out long against overwhelming numbers. Unless help came from outside, and soon, the besieged inhabitants of Brookfield would be doomed. Although Ephraim Curtis had just returned from a hard fight with the Indians, he volunteered to mount his horse again and go for aid. Henry Young, another brave man, joined him, and the two men galloped off, heading eastward for Marlborough. But they had not gone far before they were turned back by the approaching Indians.

The Nipmucks, wildly incensed that some of their intended victims had escaped and had returned to Brookfield in time to warn the inhabitants, swarmed out of the woods. They saw the abandoned houses, and in the barnyards and back lots the livestock of the settlers—cows placidly chewing their cuds, heavy-horned oxen flicking off flies with their long tails, pigs grunting contentedly in their wallows, and chickens pecking and fluffing up their feathers in the dust.

Monoco and Muttaump's warriors fell upon this peaceful rural scene with savage destruction. Listening in the garrison house, the people could hear the repeated crack of gunfire, the squeals of the pigs, and the agonized bawling of the cows and their calves. After having dispatched nearly all of the animals in sight, the Indians put the torch to the houses and barns. The wooden buildings, tinder-dry after two months of summer heat, quickly caught fire. Looking grimly down the barrels of their guns out of the windows and loopholes of the garrison, the settlers could see their cherished homes being rapidly consumed by the flames.

But there was no time for them to despair over the loss of everything they possessed. There was seldom time in a frontiersman's life to bemoan the loss of anything. The defenders could now see the Indians sneaking around the garrison house, some crouched and ready to fire at the first man who exposed himself. They could be seen in the distance, too, stamping and leaping around the meetinghouse, which they had spared to use as the headquarters of their camp.

Then night fell, and Henry Young became the first victim when he was shot and mortally wounded while peering out a garret window. Samuel Pritchard took the risk of venturing out to obtain some needed articles in a nearby building, and never came back. He was shot, and his head was cut off and mounted on a pole that was set up in full view of the horrified defenders. Thomas Wilson made a vain attempt to fetch water from the well. Shot in the jaw, he managed to stagger back into the garrison, where the women ministered as best they could to yet another wounded man who was bedded down with those who had suffered wounds in the ambush.

There was no lusty crowing of roosters the next morning to tell the Brookfield colonists that the light of another day was breaking. Cramped together in the Ayres house, they heard instead the Indians howling like a pack of hungry wolves closing in for the kill. But the Nipmucks were held off by the fire that spurted from loopholes in the four walls. The horror of their situation had steadied the hands of the men who aimed carefully through the holes in the thick wooden walls. It had steeled their nerves and sharpened their vision, especially for quick sighting of a painted brown body. The Brookfield men were fighting to save their wives and children from the terrible fate of falling into Indian hands.

The attempt to rush the garrison house and force their way in proved costly to the Nipmucks. Many of them were killed, while only a few of the English were wounded. Now the Indians resorted to fiendish ingenuity. Arrowheads that had been wrapped in hemp, soaked with oil and ignited, were sent winging toward the garrison walls. Again and again the house was the target of these blazing arrows, and it was in the act of quenching the fires that some of the defenders were wounded.

Another terrifying day passed, the light slowly fading around the scarred walls. Inside, the plight of those who fought and prayed was so desperate that they knew their store of ammunition would not last much longer. The people were suffering horribly from hunger and thirst, too, and the men were so weary that the last resources of their strength had to be drawn upon to keep the muskets steady at the loopholes and their aim unwavering. That night, brave Ephraim Curtis crept out on his hands and knees, and under cover of darkness succeeded in crawling safely through the encirclement of Indians. Once clear of them, the hardy scout broke into a run for Marlborough thirty miles away.

It happened that a man from Springfield named Judah Trumble had been approaching Brookfield the day before and had seen the flames of the burning houses from afar. He had turned his horse about and raced back to Springfield with word of what he had recognized as an Indian attack. Preparations for the relief of the stricken settlement were made at once, and couriers were sent to Hartford and Boston with the news. In Marlborough the inhabitants heard graphic details of the tragedy from Curtis and sent swift riders to enlist the aid of Major Simon Willard, who was at Lancaster with a strong detachment of troopers.

The people at Brookfield knew nothing of these developments, and the next morning the Nipmucks were back at the siege, yelling fiendishly and jockeying for the chance to storm the garrison. As the day wore on, a sudden lull in the shooting and the devilish whooping of the foe came as an ominous sign.

The Nipmucks, tired of the siege and angered by the stubborn resistance of the defenders, had withdrawn to their camp. Presently, the exhausted inmates of the garrison house heard them returning with a great clatter, and with shrieks and shouts of glee. Then from the loopholes the terrified men and women saw what the Indians had been up to.

They were pulling a two-wheeled oxcart piled high with flax, the resinous branches of pines and firs, and other combustible materials. Lashed to the tongue of the cart were a number of long spliced poles. It was only too clear what the Nipmucks intended to do. Certain doom seemed to await the defenders, for there was no water left to pour upon the flaming mass that would soon come rolling up to the front wall of the wooden building in which they were huddled.

Suddenly the sky darkened. Distant thunder rumbled. The Indians applied a torch to the inflammable stuff in the cart. At once the dry, resin-filled boughs began to crackle and take flame. In the sudden glare, the besieged colonists saw the naked braves take hold of the long end of the pole and push the burning mass toward the garrison. With fascinated horror that paralyzed their trigger fingers, the men at the loopholes watched the fire cart gain speed on its own momentum. In a moment it would be spraying flames and spewing burning twigs over the entire face of the building. Then, unbelievably and mercifully, the heavens opened!

No one had noticed the gathering thunderheads. No one had expected such miraculous answer to prayer. But there before the astonished gaze of the intended victims was the rain falling in torrents. The downpour also quenched the zeal of the Nipmucks for roasting the settlers alive. Then came another answer to prayer.

Forty-eight horsemen galloped up as the rain began to slacken. Major Simon Willard had come with his troopers at lathering speed ahead of the force that was on the way from Hartford. The men were off their mounts and inside the garrison before the Indians had recovered their wits.

The next day the sun rose in a clear sky. The weary and thankful men and women inside the bullet-splintered house stretched their stiff limbs, and listened. Could that be a cock crowing in the distance? Perhaps. They could have heard it from far away in the stillness of that morning, for the Nipmucks had vanished into the wilderness to the north.

6 Terror on the Frontier

It soon became apparent to the dazed inhabitants of Brookfield that there was nothing left of their once peaceful farming community to return to—nothing but the stark ruins of burned-out houses, the chimneys standing grotesquely above charred shells and broken walls. Their first concern was to remove the wounded to towns where they could be given medical attention. Captain Hutchinson was taken to Marlborough, and died there five days later. Captain Wheeler recovered. Major Willard stayed on in Brookfield until it was decided to abandon the settlement, and the homeless people dispersed to find refuge with families in other towns.

All trace of Philip had been lost. There were various reports and rumors of his whereabouts, but none could be verified. The truth was that, as far as anyone knew for certain, the Wampanoag sachem had vanished. But it was the horrors of Brookfield rather than Philip's disappearance that the settlers talked about most and with shuddering anxiety. Nowhere were they so gripped by fear and tension as in the settlements along the upper Connecticut River to the west of Brookfield—in the villages strung out from Northfield to Springfield. This was the Bay Colony's far-flung frontier, separated from the rest of Massachusetts by a vast stretch of wilderness.

Knowing how extremely vulnerable these little towns were, the military authorities rushed troops to Hadley, which was located halfway up the valley in a bend of the river that afforded easy access to both banks. Companies from Massachusetts and Connecticut, along with Mohegan Indians, were concentrated here.

On the first day of September, the Indians whooped into Deerfield, killed a man, and burned some dwellings. Warned of the enemy's approach, the inhabitants had fled to the safety of the garrison house. The Indians did not stop to lay siege to this fortified building, but sped on fifteen miles up the river to the tiny settlement of Northfield. Its scattered houses were burned, and eight luckless settlers who had not reached a rough stockade in time were killed.

Down the river in Hadley, preparations were being made to send provisions and troops to Northfield on the day it was destroyed. Unaware of what had happened there, Captain Richard Beers rode off the next day with thirty-six mounted men and a supply train. Progress was slow along the deeply rutted trail that wound through unbroken forest.

Early in the morning of September 4, the relief force was fording a stream within a few miles of its destination when a burst of gunfire exploded from an Indian ambuscade along the steep bank above the brook. The men fought their way out of the depression to the high ground above, and here the slaughter was swift and terrible. Captain Beers and four of his men succeeded in reaching a hill (known later as Beers Mountain) where they fought until they were felled by the foe's bullets. The wounded and the slain had to be left to the exultant Indians, and from the abandoned oxcarts they obtained a supply of ammunition and a keg of rum. It was a victory that they celebrated by getting drunk, decapitating the dead Englishmen, and impaling the severed heads on poles.

The few survivors straggled back to Hadley with news of the tragic disaster, and Major Robert Treat, commander of the Connecticut troops, left the next day with one hundred men, and successfully evacuated the Northfield settlers. Both the soldiers and the colonists they had rescued were badly shaken by the sight of the mounted English heads the Indians had set up near the trail leading to Northfield.

Meanwhile, reinforcements, including Captain Samuel Moseley's company, had arrived at military headquarters in Hadley, and with both soldiers and refugees swelling the population, the need for more food had become acute. In Deerfield, the ripened corn had been gathered and stacked in the north meadows. Captain Thomas Lathrop and Moseley were scouting around the settlement, and now it was decided to send Lathrop there with his troops to load the grain in sacks and bring it down the valley to Hadley prior to evacuating the town. On the morning of the eighteenth, his force of ninety young men, and the teamsters in charge of the heavily loaded carts, set out.

No Indians had been seen recently, and the Englishmen were in good spirits. The carts lumbered slowly over the rough road, and as the sun climbed high the warmth and beauty of the early autumn day lulled everyone with a false sense of security. It was difficult to think of danger on such a day with the mellow sunlight filtering through a golden screen of turning maple leaves, and with purple grapes hanging ripe from the wild vines. Some of the soldiers laid their muskets on the cartloads. They sang, joked, and loitered to pluck and eat grapes.

There were no scouts ranging ahead and no flankers scouring the woods to the right and the left. There was no thought of peril even when the men reached the edge of a morass where the road sloped down and passed over a marsh, made by the waters of Muddy Brook. Unaccountably, they failed to recognize it as the kind of trap that seemed to be everywhere at hand for the concealment of the foe, and into which Englishmen had already fallen at the cost of their lives.

Eagle-eyed Indian scouts had been watching the unwary soldiers. Now a large body of Nipmucks, aided by Indians from the lesser tribes of Pocumtucks and Squakeags, and led by Monoco and Sagamore Sam, lay hidden in the swamp and surrounding woods. Lathrop's troops were marching so leisurely that when they heard the first chilling yells they were spread out in a long straggling line. As the Indians sprang from their ambush and fell upon the convoy in close assault, the Englishmen jumped for whatever cover was available. Some climbed up trees, hoping to hide themselves in the leafy branches. But they were shot down like squirrels. One man of great strength clubbed his way out with the stock of his musket. Another, after being wounded in the leg, escaped by crawling under some thick bushes at the edge of the brook. Only a third of the total force survived to return to Hadley and tell the tragic story.

The waters of Muddy Brook (thereafter known as Bloody Brook) and the adjacent ground had been reddened that day with the blood of Captain Lathrop and some of the finest young men in the army—the "very flower of the County of Essex."

Having heard of the attack from a soldier who escaped, Captain Moseley and his company hastened to the scene; but they were too late to do more than drive off the Indians who were looting the corpses. After burying the English dead, Moseley led his troops to Deerfield, where they were soon joined by a relief force from Hadley under Major Treat. On their flight northward, some of the Indians stopped opposite the town, and from across the river flaunted caps, jackets, and shirts that they had stripped from their victims at Muddy Brook. Deerfield, like nearby Northfield and Brookfield to the southeast, was abandoned, and its people were scatterd in communities farther down the valley.

In Boston the commissioners of the United Colonies conferred upon the difficult problems of the war, and decided to order a new levy of men that would raise the combined force to one thousand. Plymouth's quota would be 158, Connecticut's 315, and Massachusetts would contribute 527. Major John Pynchon, prominent merchant and civic leader of Springfield, became the newly appointed commander of all the forces in western Massachusetts, and it was decided to place at least 500 men under him in that critical area.

With the abandonment of three settlements, there now remained only five inhabited villages in the upper Connecticut Valley—Hatfield, Hadley, Northampton, Westfield, and Springfield, with a population of more than 500. On October 4, all the troops assembled here marched off to join the army at Hadley. The following day Pynchon left to take command of these combined forces and to lead them against a large Indian encampment that reportedly lay some miles to the north. The major would never again see his prosperous valley town as he had left it—upon his return he would look with stricken eyes upon little more than the smoking ruins of the settlers' houses and barns.

With the departure of the troops, Springfield was left to its own defense—and with an Indian village called Long Hill located near the riverbank just a mile below the town. It was true that there had never been any trouble—that for forty years relations between the English and their Indian neighbors had been friendly. Even after Brookfield's harrowing experience with its "friendly" Indians, there were men in Springfield who refused to doubt the loyalty of the local natives.

But late in the night of the day on which the troops departed, messengers from Windsor, Connecticut, arrived in Springfield and sped through the dark streets, knocking loudly on doors, and hurriedly giving the startled householders a fearful warning. An Indian named Toto had revealed to an English family in Windsor a plot hatched by the Springfield natives. For some time they had been harboring numerous hostile Indians at Long Hill. Now, with the English soldiers gone, the opportunity to attack the town had come.

The authorities in Springfield lost no time in sending their own messenger posthaste to Hadley with the terrifying news, and the townspeople hastened to seek safety in one or another of the three fortified houses in the town.

There were a few, however, who could not believe that the Indians they had known so well and had trusted for so long were now their vengeful enemies. Lieutenant Thomas Cooper had such faith in their loyalty that he fearlessly rode off at daybreak, accompanied by Constable Thomas Miller, to investigate the situation in their village. The two trusting men had gone but a short distance when several shots were fired at them from the woods "by those bloody and deceitful monsters." Miller was instantly killed. Though mortally wounded, Lieutenant Cooper managed to cling to his saddle and turn his horse back toward the nearest garrison house. Here he gave the warning with his last breath, and slumped over dead.

Minutes later a rising chorus of savage yells was heard, and hordes of Indians swarmed into the town. They held back from an attack upon the garrisons, and instead dispersed in groups to pillage and burn the unoccupied houses. The largest single loss, and the "saddest to behold," was suffered by the Reverend Peletiah Glover, whose valuable collection of books was destroyed along with everything else he possessed.

The looting and destruction continued unabated until midafternoon when the approach of Major Pynchon with a relief force of 200 men sent the Indians scampering off into the deep woods.

Among the disconsolate inhabitants and soldiers

who were now crowded together in the garrisons and the few houses left standing, none was more down-hearted than John Pynchon. He not only saw the wide-spread destruction of property, including his own house and gristmill, but the ultimate futility of his efforts over many years to promote good relations with the Indians at Long Hill. And it was in a mood close to despair that he reflected upon the failures and blun-derings of the military forces and their leaders. Feeling that he was "more and more unfit and almost con-founded" in his "understanding," Pynchon asked to be relieved of his command. The request was granted, and Captain Samuel Appleton was appointed to suc-ceed him.

Pynchon and the rest of the colonists in towns throughout New England had good reason to feel baffled and racked with agonizing anxiety. Brave men had gone into the army who would never come back, but the sacrifice of their lives had won no victories. Philip, the archenemy, had escaped with ease, first from Mount Hope and then from Pocasset Swamp. And from Pocasset to Springfield, the military record of the English forces was strewn with galling defeats at the hands of an enemy who had skipped nimbly from town to town, and from ambush to ambush, leaving death and destruction in his wake.

The colonists had not been prepared for a war that had broken out suddenly and had spread rapidly. From the very start of the uprising, it had imposed hardships and hazards difficult to cope with. In the farming communities of all the colonies, the men had to provide a living for their families and, at the same time, protection from the Indians who seemed to lurk everywhere and who struck without warning. Many settlers had been murdered in their fields while engaged in the plowing, the sowing, and the reaping that had to be done.

Men were needed for military service, too, and they had to give time to the building of additional fortifications and garrison houses that all the towns were now making frantic haste to get ready for their defense. Growing crops on many farms, particularly those around the abandoned towns, had been left to the Indians, and what they failed to take or destroy was usually ruined by roaming cattle. Loss of the harvests, for all these reasons, resulted in a growing shortage of food for both people and livestock. And the Indians never lost a chance to destroy the mills and break up the millstones, knowing that in each town the colonists depended upon the local mill to grind their grain.

But it was the abysmal failure of the war effort that had an almost paralyzing effect upon the people. The fate of the Connecticut Valley towns that had borne the brunt of Indian fury was a grim forecast of what could be expected at any time in other areas. The army and its leaders were fighting an enemy whose strategy and tactics were foreign to the Englishmen's concept of how a war should properly be fought. They clung to the European idea that a well-drilled army should go out in close formation to look for the enemy and to engage him in battle. But there were no battle-fields in New England. There were dense forests and miry swamps and innumerable streams of all sizes, and the Indians were amazingly adept at using them to advantage.

The English were incredibly slow in adapting their tactics to the conditions of forest warfare in which they had to match wits and methods with a wily foe. With the experiences of Beers, Hutchinson, and Lathrop in mind, perhaps, Governor Leverett urged that the soldiers "be commanded to attend the enemy's method, which is the best way of fighting him in this brushy wilderness."

It was a war, though, in which good scouting was of primary importance, and the English soldiers had neither the necessary skill in tracking nor adequate knowledge of the "brushy wilderness." In their movements through the forests, the English needed friendly Indians to use as scouts. Unfortunately, the unprovoked attack upon Hutchinson and Wheeler near Brookfield by supposedly neutral Nipmucks, and the devastation of Springfield a few weeks later by hitherto friendly Indian neighbors, so alarmed the colonists that they became almost hysterically suspicious of all Indians. The General Court in Boston ordered:

That no person shall entertain, own, or countenance any Indian, under penalty of being a betrayer of his government.

That a guard be set at the entrance of the town of Boston,

and that no Indian be suffered to enter, upon any pretense, without a guard of two musketeers, and not to lodge in town.

The most relentless and brutal persecution of various Indian groups living in Plymouth and Massachusetts under English jurisdiction followed. Among them were the Praying Indians, and John Eliot pleaded in vain for their protection against needless cruelties. During the autumn of 1675, several hundred of his converts, including women, children, and old men, were transported to barren, windswept Deer Island in Boston Harbor, where they were left to shift for themselves. Here, and on Clark's Island in Plymouth Harbor, these unfortunate victims of war hysteria suffered from lack of adequate clothing and shelter, and from a diet of little more than clams and shellfish. For trying to help them in small ways, Eliot and his co-worker Daniel Gookin were reviled and their lives threatened.

On the other hand, Captain Samuel Moseley became something of a hero to everyone who hated the loyal Indians. His own hatred of them was so intense that his record as a brave soldier was marred by his many acts of flagrant cruelty to these inoffensive natives.

There were no Praying Indians among the Mohegans and Pequots in Connecticut, and these tribes remained loyal allies of the English throughout the war. Some of them were nearly always with the Connecticut forces wherever they fought. In time, Massachusetts and Plymouth came to see the folly of the

harsh treatment of their own loyal Indians, and in the
later stages of the war enlisted them as scouts and
soldiers.

It was a tribute to John Eliot, and other selfless missionaries, that many of the converted Indians who had
been grievously mistreated gave efficient service to the
colonial armies when the authorities turned to them
for help. Daniel Gookin maintained that they "turned
ye balance to ye English side so that ye enemy went
down ye wind amain."

But the balance in that fall of 1675 was all on the
side of the copper-skinned warriors who padded silently and swiftly along shadowed trails in the deep
woods, emerging again and again to set towns aflame
and to strike down settlers and soldiers. With terror
stalking the colonies, another New England autumn
came and passed. Trees lost their gold and scarlet
leaves, and the Indians lost cover for their ambuscades.
The tribes went their separate ways to hole in for the
season when the land would be lashed by cutting winds
and buried under snowfalls.

Somewhere in one of those winter hide-outs, King
Philip himself must have taken shelter. He had become a kind of mystery leader whose movements and
activities were cloaked in darkest secrecy. Did the
sachems and sagamores of other tribes listen to him
around the council fires and take orders from him?
Did he work feverishly at coordinating the war efforts
of the various groups, seeking to weld together all the
tribes in a powerful Indian confederacy? And had he

participated in some of the assaults upon the English?

The answers to these questions can be nothing more than conjectures. What is known is that the Wampanoag sachem had dared to take the initiative in rebelling against the dominance of the white men. And with his success in escaping their clutches in Pocasset Swamp and in drawing the Nipmucks into the war as allies, Philip had reawakened Indian pride and had raised Indian hopes of wiping out the English to the last man. The crucial question now was: Would the Narragansetts remain neutral, or would they throw their considerable weight on Philip's side?

7 The Great Swamp Fight

The Narragansetts had as many warriors as the combined forces of the Wampanoags and the Nipmucks, and the strategic advantage of being in a location from which they could strike northward into Massachusetts or westward into Connecticut. As Philip's successes mounted, the United Colonies had watched ever more fearfully to see what the Narragansetts would do. Further efforts had been made to strengthen the agreement reached with some of their representatives in July, and in the middle of October a new treaty was signed. Again the Narragansetts promised to keep peace with the English, and pledged themselves to bring into Boston on or before October 28 every Indian fugitive in their country.

That not one was brought in then or later probably surprised no one, for the authorities had been gathering intelligence that gave them reason to suspect the Narragansetts of treachery. Not only had they failed to keep the twice-made promise to hand over enemy Indians, but it appeared that their warriors had already been engaged in attacks upon the English. The most alarming information came from an Indian who, upon his return to Plymouth from a visit with the Narragansetts, declared that many Wampanoags were sharing winter quarters with them and that Canonchet, a young and powerful sachem, was planning to become Philip's ally the following spring. This was the last straw for the United Colonies. "The Narragansetts do but juggle with us," they bitterly decided.

The prospect of the involvement in King Philip's War of a thousand warriors of this strongest of all the tribes raised weighty questions for the commissioners at their session early in November. Could they afford to wait until spring before taking any decisive action? To delay would give the Indians the advantage of concealment in leafy woods. On the other hand, dared they take the risk of sending an army out into the wilderness on a winter campaign against a hidden foe?

It was already evident that winter was coming early that year. There could be no assurance of protection for the troops in bitter cold; forest paths might be obliterated by snow, and supply lines could be cut off if the rivers and harbors froze.

On November 12, the commissioners made their desperate decision. Faced with what they saw as the alternative of destroying or being destroyed, they voted to raise a thousand men for an expeditionary force, and appointed Governor Josiah Winslow of Plymouth commander in chief. By a tactful request, they secured the cooperation of Rhode Island to the extent that Governor William Coddington promised to provide boats for transporting men and supplies.

With so much at stake, the commissioners and government officials laid careful plans, and began preparations at once for the expedition. Each of the three colonies had its quota of men to raise, their "ablest and most suitable" for such a difficult undertaking. Millers ground hundreds of bushels of grain, and bakers worked overtime making bread. And vast quantities of powder, lead, bullets, and flints were collected and stored.

December 2 was officially designated as a day of humiliation and prayer for the success of the perilous venture. Throughout the colonies, people came to their meetinghouses to find strength and comfort in the words of their pastors, who urged them to be calm and courageous and who fervently invoked God's aid and blessing. Within the next few days, the soldiers said goodbye to their families and, accompanied by chaplains and surgeons, moved out upon the roads, the Plymouth men heading for their assembly point at Taunton, the Massachusetts troops for Dedham, and those in Connecticut for New London.

By the ninth, both the Massachusetts and Plymouth forces had arrived in Rehoboth. Major Appleton, who had returned from service in the Connecticut Valley, was there in command of the Bay Colony's 540 men, and with him were captains Moseley, James Oliver, Isaac Johnson, Nathaniel Davenport, and Joseph Gardiner, and Captain Prentice at the head of a troop of cavalry. Major William Bradford commanded the Plymouth force of 158 men.

Benjamin Church had come out of retirement, and at this crucial time was eager to offer his services. General Winslow had urged him to take command of a company, but Church preferred the freedom of being on his own to track down the enemy. So the general gave him a staff position as special assistant.

There was no delay at Rehoboth, and Winslow saw his army safely ferried across the Seekonk River to Providence. Rhode Island had assisted in the embarkation by sending several vessels to meet the needs of the troops. A rapid overland march brought them to their advance base at the village of Wickford, Rhode Island, which was located beside a small harbor on the western shore of Narragansett Bay. Richard Smith had a garrison and trading post here, and other houses stood nearby.

While awaiting word from Major Robert Treat, who was on the way with his Connecticut troops, small scouting parties went out from Wickford to comb the surrounding woods in search of Indians. Benjamin Church had been among the first to reach the base camp, and he was the first to take off into the forest with a volunteer group of "brisk blades" to hunt the enemy. On a frosty night, in moonlight bright enough to discern human forms crouched behind leafless bushes, they captured eighteen Indians and brought them to headquarters as a "present for General Winslow." Other scouting parties, one led by the commander himself, came back with prisoners, too, and reports of having burned a number of wigwams. All except one of the Indian captives were transported for temporary safekeeping to Aquidneck Island. The one exception was a Narragansett named Peter, who was a prize catch.

The young Indian had been caught while running away from the secret fortified village the Narragansetts had built on a small island in the middle of the Great Swamp. Something had happened back there that had so enraged Peter that he had deserted his people. He had rushed out into the night alone, and when he was picked up by the English troops he offered to lead them to the Narragansett stronghold. Perhaps Chief Canonchet, angered by some infraction of Indian law, had given Peter a stern reprimand or had meted out severe punishment. Whatever it was, the deserter kept it to himself. But he readily answered General Winslow's questions. No one listened more attentively than Benjamin Church, and as he closely observed the Indian's dark face he decided that Peter could be trusted.

By now the Narragansetts were, of course, well aware of the presence of the English forces at Wickford, and in no doubt about what they intended to do. But the enemy, feeling safe in what with reason he believed to be an impregnable position, knew nothing about the defection to the English of the disgruntled Peter. Early in the day of the fifteenth another Narragansett, known to the white men as Stonewall John, appeared at General Winslow's headquarters, ostensibly to negotiate for peace. It soon developed that he had nothing important to discuss, and suspecting that he had come to spy on his camp, Winslow dismissed him, saying, "Go tell your sachems to come and talk peace with me."

Stonewall John had not come alone, and immediately after his departure a group of warriors who had lain concealed near the garrison opened fire on Captain Gardiner's company and killed three of the men. Before the troops could drive off the Indians, two of Captain Oliver's men were also slain.

Major Treat had not yet arrived with his Connecticut contingent, and with the passing of precious time, Winslow was becoming increasingly worried and impatient. No replenishment of provisions had come from Massachusetts, and there was now only a scant supply of food left. Moreover, the weather looked threatening, and a severe storm could be disastrous to the expedition. A detail of Captain Prentice's horse-men was sent down to Pettaquamscut on the sixteenth in the hope of learning that Major Treat had come that way and was ready to join the main army. But the troopers rode back with nothing but gloomy news.

Pettaquamscut was a small settlement about eight miles south of Wickford, and the point from which Winslow planned to march westward to the Great Swamp. The main house was Jireh Bull's large stone garrison, in which seventeen people were sheltered on the night of the fifteenth. No watch had been set, and in the darkness Indians crept close, forced the doors, and massacred all but two of the inmates. When Prentice's troopers came upon the scene the next day, they found the garrison house reduced to a smoking ruin.

Good news was received, though, on the day follow-ing their return when word came from Major Treat that he had reached Pettaquamscut with his men. Winslow's spirits rose, for now his force would be augmented by 315 English troops and 150 Mohegans and Pequots. Preparations to break camp started at once, and on the eighteenth all the Massachusetts and Plymouth troops except the few who remained to guard Smith's garrison left Wickford, and marched down to join the Connecticut soldiers.

There had been a heavy fall of snow, and on that cold, overcast day, the men got ready to camp for the night at Pettaquamscut by building fires around the charred ruins of the garrison house. After a meager supper, they lay down on the snow-covered ground, huddling together for warmth and drawing their long woolen coats close around their shivering limbs, for they had neither tents nor blankets for protection from the bitter weather. It could not have been a restful night, and the soldiers were undoubtedly glad to get up at daybreak and stamp the numbness out of their legs and feet.

Whatever the cost of the desperate gamble might be, General Winslow was now ready for a decisive encounter with the Narragansetts on that wintry morning of December 19. The order to march was given, and the men took their places in the long column, knowing with the grim acceptance of brave soldiers that a hideous ordeal lay ahead. They knew that in all probability many of them would not live to return, but they plodded out resolutely through the deep snow, shouldering their muskets and carrying ammunition and a scant ration of food.

Captain Moseley led off with his company, guided by the Indian Peter, and the rest of the Massachusetts units followed behind. Next came General Winslow on horseback with the Plymouth men, and Major Treat brought up the rear with his Connecticut contingents. Strung out like a black ribbon across the snowy landscape, the winding column moved on westward. In that winter wasteland, there was no visible trail to follow, but Peter guided them with unerring Indian instinct, and a little after noon the forward troops reached the dark rim of the swamp. It was not only good fortune for the English that they had Peter to guide them; in addition, the intense cold had frozen the watery terrain and thereby given them a firm footing. Otherwise, they might have bogged down disastrously in the muck and the mire.

Advancing rapidly over the crunchy ground, the Massachusetts men came suddenly upon the walled Indian village that had been built upon an elevation extending over five or six acres. Some Indians fenced in their villages with a stockade of logs set on end, but the English had never before seen such fortifications as the Narragansetts had erected here. The palisade itself was unusually stout and strong, and around it was a great rampart of brush, and the limbs and branches of trees were piled high and deep. All approaches to the fort were protected, too, by blockhouses from which the defenders could fire upon an assault force. Within the walls, perhaps as many as 3,500 Indians, counting the women and children, were sheltered in crowded wigwams.

Either by chance or guided by Peter, the first of the English troops to arrive came upon the one weak section in the defenses. Here the palisade had not been completed, and the gap had been bridged by a large tree trunk laid horizontally across the opening. It had the protection, though, of a blockhouse.

There was but one way to begin the attack upon the fort—by a concerted rush at this entrance. And with supreme heroism the leading companies of Massachusetts soldiers made it. They swept across the frozen ground and charged the gap, struggling valiantly to get across the log and into the fort. Inevitably, many of them did not succeed. The Narragansetts and Wampanoags had not been caught off guard. From the blockhouse they raked the English with musket fire, and Captain Isaac Johnson, along with some of his men, fell dead at the entrance. Captain Nathaniel Davenport gained the fort only to face a withering volley from within that killed him and wounded many of the soldiers in his company.

Momentarily confused and disorganized, the survivors fell back, but with the reinforcements that Moseley and Gardiner brought up, the troops rushed the entrance of the fort once more. In that second assault Captain Joseph Gardiner was shot dead. But the men were heartened by a rallying cry from Major Appleton, who reached the scene with the rest of the Massachusetts troops. "They run! They run!" he cried in a booming voice that must have startled the Indians. And on a wave of fresh courage the massed soldiers stormed over the tree trunk and into the fort.

The breach in the wall was undefended when the companies of Plymouth and Connecticut troops arrived at the fort, for the Indians in the blockhouse had fled. But sharpshooters from other vantage points took the lives of three Connecticut captains—John Gallop, Samuel Marshall, and Nathaniel Seeley—and Captain John Mason was mortally wounded.

Some distance outside the fort, General Winslow and his staff received reports from messengers, conferred with officers, and listened to the uproar of the battle and the yells and war whoops of the Indians that resounded through the swamp. Benjamin Church did not like his passive role of aide to the general. At last he could no longer restrain his impatience over being out of the action. With General Winslow's permission, he hastened to the fort with a small group that had volunteered to go with him. Near the entrance they saw the bodies of the Englishmen who had been shot down in the initial assaults upon the fort grotesquely sprawled in death, some lying in the tangled branches of the felled trees on both sides of the log. Everywhere the white ground was stained with the blood of the fallen.

The battle was still raging when Benjamin Church entered the fort, but he quickly saw that the English, fighting like demons with swords and muskets and pistols, were rapidly overpowering the Indian warriors. It was a weird scene of horrible carnage in the fading light of the short winter day.

The dead, the dying, and the wounded lay in such heaps around the wigwams, and in the narrow spaces between, that those who still carried on the desperate struggle had to step warily to keep from falling over them. There were so many more brown-skinned bodies among the slain that it was evident that the English soldiers had wreaked a terrible vengeance upon their foes. No one among them had shouted "Remember Bloody Brook!" but memories of those autumn weeks when the whole valley of the Connecticut River had run red with English blood burned in their thoughts, and gave a terrifying strength to arms that slashed the warriors and clubbed them mercilessly with gunstocks when powder and bullets were spent.

Seeing that the Indians had hacked openings in the palisade that they might fight to better advantage in the surrounding swamp, and make their escape into the woods beyond when forced to flee, Church and his men picked up a bloody track and hastened in pursuit.

Outside, the warriors were discovered leaping from tree to tree, and climbing up into the branches to fire down upon the English troops inside the fort. At once, several of them became easy targets for the Indian fighter who could leap as nimbly as the best of them, and whose shots were usually more accurate than theirs. Sharp-eyed Benjamin Church singled out a small group moving toward the breached walls. Taking advantage of a pile of brush, he and his men dropped down behind this cover to wait for them to come within musket range. Unaware that they were being watched, the Indians crawled nearer to the fort.

"Now, brave boys," Church said softly to his companions, "if we mind our hits we may have a brave shot, and let our sign for firing on them be their rising to their feet."

It was not long before the Indians rose up as one man, intending to pour a volley into the fort. On the instant, Church's group went into action. They "gave them such a round volley that those who escaped with their lives were so amazed that they scampered they knew not whither themselves." The survivors jumped over a log and into the fort, and burrowed into an empty wigwam.

With their guns reloaded, Church and his men charged the wigwam, intending to overturn it as they would a chicken coop. But some of the Indians had recovered their balance and their courage by the time the Englishmen reached the hut, for Church himself suddenly saw, too late, the muzzles of their guns pointed at him through a hole in the wall. Before he could spring to safety, three bullets fired in quick succession struck him in three places. One ripped through his breeches, grazing the flesh. Another harmlessly pierced a pocket. But the third lodged in his thigh, inflicting a painful wound.

Nerved for action, Church refused the help of his men, and insisted on remaining in the thick of the fight as long as he was able to stand. He particularly wanted to finish the job of routing from their shelter the Indians who had fired upon him. But at that moment he discovered smoke billowing from a number of wigwams. He frowned as he saw the flames spurt upward and heard the piercing screams of the Indians trapped inside.

Benjamin Church was never guilty of wanton cruelty, but it was not out of mercy for those who were being roasted alive that he cried out to the soldiers around him, "Stop it! Stop this madness! Save the wigwams!" He knew that the enemy's supplies of food were stored there. Great wooden tubs and baskets filled with corn, cured venison, dried fish, and other provisions lined the walls and made the wigwams bulletproof. Here was food in plenty for the famished army, as well as warm shelter for the able and the disabled during that winter night. It was almost dark, and snow had begun to fall again. Church could imagine the horror of a march back to headquarters through the blinding snow. He pleaded with the soldiers to check the flames. "Orders from the general," they shouted as they sped away to set more wigwams on fire.

With blood dripping from his wound, Church hastened outside to where General Winslow sat on his horse. Most urgently, he explained why the wigwams should be spared. But there were other advisers who thought only of destroying the enemy's winter food supply. It was to them that the general listened.

So Benjamin Church stood there in the falling snow and watched the holocaust across the broken walls of the fort. Black smoke rolled up higher and higher above the glare of the inferno below. Gradually the cries of the victims grew fainter and fainter, and soon there were no sounds except the crackling of burning timbers and the scattered volleys that for a while were exchanged between the pursued and the pursuers. At this moment of victory for the English, the Indians were not curdling the blood with their fiendish yells. Canonchet and other Narragansett sachems had fled the scene where so many of their warriors, and their women and children, lay dead, and with the rest of the survivors were plunging deeper and deeper into the still woods.

But there could be no certainty that the vanquished foe would not return to renew the attack upon Winslow's troops if they remained long in the burned-out fort. This was emphasized in the discussion of what course of action to take. Church argued that it would be far better to camp in the Indian village, giving the bone-weary soldiers the rest they needed, and to place the wounded in the shelter of the blockhouses. Whether or not it was good advice that should have been acted upon can be only a matter of speculation. Church was again overruled by other advisers, and General Winslow decided to march back to his main base at Wickford, since there was almost no shelter at Pettaquamscut.

About four o'clock in the afternoon the exhausted troops staggered out of the smoldering fort. Somehow they found strength to throw off the dead weight of torpor, and to follow blindly the marching orders of their officers. Somehow crude litters had been made for those too critically wounded to walk or to be carried on horseback. But there was neither time nor strength to give to the dead. They had to be left there, buried under the snow.

That the men who marched the eighteen miles back to Richard Smith's garrison house at Wickford that night did not succumb in the storm-racked forest was another kind of victory. Fatigued from lack of food and from marching and fighting, they stumbled and fell in the heavy snowdrifts that blocked the way. They were so weary that they did not trouble to lift aching arms to push back the icy branches that raked their faces. Most of them were so miserably cold and sleepy that there was the added danger that they would choose to lie down and freeze to death. For the wounded it was an even more terrible nightmare of agony, and twenty of them died on the way back.

At two o'clock in the morning the main body of troops reeled into the camp they had left soon after dawn the previous day. General Winslow and a group of forty men had become separated from the others in the dark and did not arrive until seven. Providentially, Captain Richard Goodale's sloop, laden with provisions for the army, had got through from Boston and was tied up at Smith's Landing, having reached Wickford the evening before.

After the dispiriting failures of the English during the spring and summer months, their victory over the Narragansetts gave the morale of New Englanders a tremendous lift. They could be justly proud, too, of both officers and men who had fought with a gallantry that would not soon be forgotten. The decisive victory they had won may well have saved the New England colonists from extermination. But it was a costly victory. The 70 men who were killed included half the company commanders, and of the 150 wounded, close to a third of them died.

On the other side, the enemy was dealt a severe blow. No reliable estimate of the number slain was

ever made, but the losses of the Narragansetts were
known to have been far greater than those of the English, and a significant loss, too, was that of the Indians'
winter food supply.

Canonchet escaped to fight again, but in the Great
Swamp Fight of December 19, 1675, the English cut
down the strength of the Narragansetts to approximately half of what it had been.

8 Towns Aflame

General Winslow had marched to the attack on the
Narragansett stronghold in the nick of time. Had he
delayed even a day or two longer he might never again
have had the opportunity. For the snowstorm that
had started in the afternoon of the nineteenth increased
in severity, and for several weeks the troops were snow-
bound in their encampment at Wickford. Fortunately,
the waters of Narragansett Bay remained open, mak-

ing it possible to evacuate the more seriously wounded men by boat to nearby Newport on Aquidneck Island, where they could be given better medical care. Benjamin Church was among them, and for several months he was inactive while recovering from his wound.

The Connecticut troops had suffered particularly heavy casualties, and with their morale at low ebb, Major Treat was allowed to take them back home to recuperate. There was nothing at Wickford to raise the spirits of the Massachusetts and Plymouth men, but they remained there and coped with the hardships as best they could. When the provisions Captain Goodale had brought were used up and no more supply vessels came with replenishments until late in January, the soldiers cheerfully turned to foraging for their food. They unearthed corn from Indian storage pits, and made nocturnal raids on the livestock of English settlers. With a pig or a goat roasting over a bed of coals inside their improvised shelters, they could forget the rigors of the weather and the perils of fighting Indians.

At his headquarters in the garrison house, Winslow chafed at the delay in taking up the pursuit of the enemy while he was still within striking distance. At the general's urging, the commissioners in Boston were making efforts to raise additional troops to reinforce the depleted army at Wickford.

Snow still lay deep in the woods and along the trails when the first recruits began to arrive. Commanded by captains Samuel Brocklebank, Joseph Sill, and Samuel Wadsworth, they reached the rendezvous about the tenth of January after a difficult march, and other Massachusetts troops soon followed. A vessel came into the harbor with supplies of food, and toward the end of the month Major Treat returned with his force, which included a number of recruits. Now that he had a sizable army again, General Winslow was ready to begin the long-delayed pursuit of the enemy.

Then, suddenly, the weather changed. Rising temperatures melted the snow and turned the frozen ground to slush. The thaw brought relief to the shivering soldiers, but it also made it easier for the Indians to outdistance their pursuers. Undeterred by this possibility, General Winslow left Wickford with his army on January 28, and marched out into the Narragansett country.

From the start it was a frustratingly futile chase. The Indians were already heading northwestward for the Nipmuck territory, and although the troops pressed hard behind, they could not overtake the main body of the fleeing Narragansetts. At times the English came upon the still-smoking embers of their campfires, but for all their efforts they succeeded only in capturing a few stragglers. As their supply of food dwindled and was consumed altogether, the troops were forced to kill and eat some of their horses, and to scrabble, as the Indians did, for the tuberous groundnuts.

It finally became obvious to Winslow that his hopes for another victory over the Narragansetts could not

be realized. Instead, his dogged pursuit of the foe came
to be ingloriously called the "hungry march." It ended
on February 3 when the general reached Marlborough
and there disbanded his footsore, hungry, and weary
men. He led most of the Plymouth and Massachusetts
companies to Boston, and Major Treat returned with
his troops to Connecticut. Captain Wadsworth, in
command of a garrison force, was left at Marlborough,
which stood on the old Bay Path and had served as a
base of operations for troops from Massachusetts in
their movements to and from the Connecticut Valley.
With the army disbanded, the towns along the frontier
to the east now became tempting targets for the
Indians.

Probably no rebellion, large or small, ever had for
its leader one who remained as shadowy as did King
Philip. For the greater part of the duration of the war
that bears his name, and which he planned and pre-
cipitated, he was a kind of ghost leader about whose
movements and leadership the English knew little or
nothing. It is fairly well established, however, that
Philip made a vain attempt to persuade the Mohawks
to join his uprising. Late in December, he and some
of his followers crossed the Berkshire Hills and, in a
native village situated about twenty miles northeast of
Albany, made contact with the Indians he tried to
inflame against the English. The Mohawks not only
refused to become involved in Philip's war, but un-
ceremoniously drove off the Wampanoag sachem and
his men.

In all likelihood they returned some time in January of 1676 to join the large concentration of Nipmucks at their main camp around Menameset on the Ware River. Other groups were congregated in villages at Quabaug near deserted Brookfield, and in the vicinity of Mount Wachusett, about twelve miles west of Lancaster. Although the Indians had obtained supplies of food from abandoned English towns, many of them had been prevented by the war from reaping their own crops, and had been driven from their fishing grounds. Moreover, the Narragansetts had lost all their winter provisions in the Great Swamp Fight, and with both the Wampanoags and the Narragansetts crowding in upon the Nipmucks in the dead of winter, the need for more food became acute.

Throughout the colonies, during the lull in the war, the people waited in nervous dread of the next savage blow, knowing it would be struck somewhere by the Indians sooner or later. The commissioners of the United Colonies were aware of the danger, and soon after General Winslow's army was demobilized, they made plans to raise a force of 600 mounted men for an offensive campaign against the Indians at Quabaug and Mount Wachusett. But, inexplicably, neither the commissioners nor Governor Leverett had heeded the warning given them as early as January 24 by a Christian Indian who had been spying in the Nipmuck country.

James Quannapohit had mingled freely with the Indians at Quabaug, pretending to be an enemy of the

English, and had learned that preparations were afoot for an attack upon the town of Lancaster, to be followed by assaults upon other settlements along the unprotected frontier. But the authorities gave little credence to the dire report, thinking perhaps that the Indians would not stir from their villages while the trees were still bare and the ground covered with snow.

At his home in Cambridge, Captain Daniel Gookin was sleeping soundly on the night of February 9 when an urgent knocking awakened him and brought him quickly to the door. He found Job Kattenanit, a second Indian spy, standing there. He had just arrived from the Nipmuck country, having traveled over eighty miles through the wilderness on snowshoes. Job wasted no words. Excitedly he blurted out the terrifying news that several hundred Indians were already on the way to attack Lancaster, expecting to reach the town the next morning. Acting upon his own initiative, Gookin at once sent mounted messengers galloping off to warn the threatened town, and to order there the troops left in Marlborough under Captain Wadsworth.

Lancaster, situated midway between Groton to the northeast and Marlborough to the southeast, was a community with five widely separated garrison houses. The principal one was the large fortified house of the pastor, Mr. Joseph Rowlandson, which stood in the center near the meetinghouse. On the fateful day of February 10, Mr. Rowlandson was in Boston, where he had gone to plead for an adequate detail of troops to protect his town.

Fortunately, most of the inhabitants were sheltered in the garrisons when, early on the morning of the tenth, the Indians came howling out of the forest, brandishing their guns and tomahawks. In the ensuing onslaught, the inmates of the Rowlandson house suffered the heaviest casualties. Completely surrounded by the attackers, the defenders kept up a desperate fight for two hours, but their doom was sealed when the Indians brought a pile of flax and hemp from the barn and set fire to the building. As the frantic people rushed out to escape the flames, the Indians fell upon them with guns and hatchets.

Pastor Rowlandson's wife reported that when she came to the door with her children, the bullets were rattling against the walls of the house as if "one had thrown a handful of stones." Her brother-in-law, a sister, and a nephew were killed, and the shot that pierced Mrs. Rowlandson's side passed through and critically wounded the little daughter in her arms. The dead and the dying lay all about, "some here, some there, like sheep torn by wolves."

Of the thirty-seven people in the pastor's house, only one man escaped. Twelve were killed, and twenty-four taken captive, including Mrs. Mary Rowlandson, with the wounded child in her arms, and two older children.

In the meantime, Captain Wadsworth was hasten-

ing with forty men from Marlborough to the relief
of the besieged inhabitants of Lancaster. Learning of
their approach, the Indians retreated, driving livestock
before them and with their prisoners in tow. The
other garrison houses had held off the enemy until
Captain Wadsworth's arrival, but so many houses and
barns had been destroyed that the town was abandoned some weeks later.

Everywhere the colonists were seized with such terror that they hardly dared leave the garrisons, and the
Massachusetts Government was bombarded with pleas
for military protection. But the presence of more than
a hundred soldiers did not save Medfield, a town located just seventeen miles southwest of Boston. All except thirty men on duty at the main garrison were
quartered in houses throughout the community rather
than in one place.

Feeling secure with so many soldiers in their midst,
the inhabitants were sleeping peacefully in their own
beds while several hundred Indians crept noiselessly
into the town sometime in the early morning hours of
February 21. Dispersing, they found cover in various
places, hiding behind orchard walls, barns, and sheds.
At daybreak, Samuel Morse went out to feed his livestock, and saw to his horror the black eyes of an Indian
peering out of a pile of hay. Returning quietly to the
house, he gathered his family in frantic haste and with
them fled toward the nearest garrison. Looking back,
he saw his barn burst into flames, and at the same time
heard the crack of musket fire from all directions.

Other farmers, up early like Samuel Morse but not so lucky, were shot, and fell dead on their doorsteps. Eighteen people were slain before the inhabitants and the soldiers reached the garrisons. Nothing could be done to save the houses, and forty or fifty, along with the barns, were burned down.

The Indians did not remain long after they heard the roar of a cannon the soldiers fired to warn the people in Dedham, which lay a few miles to the northeast. Loaded with loot, the marauders streaked off in a northwesterly direction, crossed a bridge that spanned the Charles River, and then stopped long enough to set fire to the bridge. Later, someone found a note they had left attached to one of the charred posts which read:

Know by this paper that the Indians that thou hast provoked to wrath and anger will war these twenty-one years if you will. We come three hundred this time and there are many Indians left. Consider, the Indians lose nothing but their lives; you must lose all your fair houses and cattle.

Mercifully, this savage violence did not continue for twenty-one years, but for many weeks there was no abatement of the wrath that took so heavy a toll of the "fair houses and cattle"—and the lives of settlers and soldiers.

In the meantime, the commissioners had gone ahead with their plans for an offensive campaign against the foe. Six hundred mounted men from Massachusetts and Connecticut were assembled and placed under the command of Major Thomas Savage. And large quantities of food, clothing, and ammunition were collected and brought to the main supply base at Marlborough.

Late in February the expedition set out hopefully from Brookfield, expecting to find the enemy in large numbers somewhere in the northern reaches of the wilderness. But the Nipmucks were not waiting for them, and the deeper the troopers penetrated the dark forests, the more perilous their situation became. Although the campaign had accomplished nothing, Major Savage sensibly decided that it was better to retreat than to risk disaster, and led his men down to Hadley. Here they dispersed, some of them finding quarters in nearby Hatfield and Northampton.

It was fortunate that Major Treat had brought two companies of his Connecticut soldiers, and Captain William Turner a company of Massachusetts men, to Northampton, for at dawn on the morning of March 14 it was attacked by a large force of Indians. Unaware of the presence of the troops, they broke through the stockade that surrounded the town and found themselves in a trap. Before they could escape, the soldiers inflicted heavy losses upon them, and for once they were forced "to fly with great confusion."

But elsewhere the Indians were wreaking havoc upon the settlements. On the thirteenth, just the day before the attack on Northampton, the notorious Nipmuck chief Monoco led a major assault on Groton, the eastern frontier town located a few miles northeast of devastated Lancaster. And, like Lancaster, Groton had to be abandoned after the destruction of most of its dwellings. The four garrison houses, in which the inhabitants had found refuge, successfully withstood the attack.

From frequent association with the English, Monoco had become fairly proficient in their language. This gave him the special advantage, and satisfaction, of being able to taunt the people in one of the garrisons while their meetinghouse burned.

"What will you do for a place to pray in," he mocked, "now that we have burned your meetinghouse? And we will burn Concord, Watertown, Cambridge, and Boston. I have 480 warriors with me. We will show you what we will do."

Meanwhile, the enemy had struck a sickening blow as far away as Plymouth. A short distance south of the town, William Clark maintained an isolated garrison house at Eel River. A Wampanoag Indian named Totoson was so well known to the Clark family that he had eaten a meal with them a few days before he repaid their friendly hospitality with a murderous attack. Early on the Sunday morning of March 12, Totoson and a group of warriors lay hidden until the men had departed for Sabbath services in Plymouth. Then the Indians emerged from their hiding place, entered the house, and killed eleven defenseless women and children. Before retiring into the woods, Totoson and his band plundered the garrison of provisions, guns, and ammunition, and set it on fire.

About the same time that this outrage was being perpetrated upon the Clark garrison house, enemy marauders in the Narragansett country burned down all the remaining houses in Warwick and Wickford. Richard Smith's garrison, which had been General Winslow's headquarters at the time of the Great Swamp Fight, had already been destroyed, and settlers throughout the area south of the Pawtuxet River had fled to Aquidneck Island.

If the birds again sang most pleasantly in that early spring of 1676, there could have been no joy in their songs, or in other voices of spring, for the distraught people of New England. For ringing in their ears were the hideous yells and war whoops that signaled death and desolation throughout the land. Everywhere there was terror as each day brought news of settlers being killed and houses burned. There were few families that had not felt the impact of grief through the loss of loved ones.

But the fate of some of those who were taken captive by the Indians was more terrible than death. The Reverend Cotton Mather reported that "those devils incarnate stripped their unhappy prisoners and caused them to run the gauntlet, and whipped them after a cruel and bloody manner. Then they threw hot ashes upon them, and, cutting off collops of flesh, they put fire into the wounds, and so, with exquisite, leisurely, horrible torments, roasted them out of the world."

9 The Death of Canonchet and the Battle of Green Hill

On the Lord's day of March 26, the congregation in the meetinghouse at Marlborough had sat down after singing a hymn. Their pastor, the Reverend William Brinsmead, stepped outside for a moment, seeking relief from a toothache. What he saw in the distance sent him racing back into the church crying, "Indians! Indians!" With that timely warning, the people were able to reach the garrison safely, but while they hud-

137

dled there in terror, the enemy fired most of the houses
and drove off the cattle. Soon afterward Marlborough
became yet another abandoned town, with the exception of the garrison, which was maintained there by
the army.

On March 26, too, a small party of settlers riding
into Springfield to attend services at the meetinghouse
there were attacked by Indians and a man and a girl
were slain. Two women, each with a small child, were
kidnaped, and when the Indians were about to be
overtaken by a company of mounted soldiers, the ab-
ductors killed the children and critically wounded the
two mothers before escaping into the forest.

That same Sunday tragedy befell a company of fifty
Plymouth soldiers and a score of friendly Indians under the command of Captain Michael Peirce. Out
scouring the country in search of the enemy, they had
spent the night of March 25 at the garrison house in
Rehoboth. Here Peirce learned of the presence of some
Indians a few miles to the north near the eastern bank
of the Pawtucket River (now the Blackstone), and the
next morning he started off, hoping to come upon
them.

The Plymouth force soon fell in with a party of Narragansetts led by Canonchet, but the Indians feigned
a retreat. The sachem had divided his warriors into
two parties, and while one group circled around the
flanks of the English and gained a favorable position,
the others, some "limping along to make believe they
were lame," lured the impetuous Captain Peirce across

the Pawtucket in pursuit. Suddenly he found himself beset by vastly superior numbers of warriors. The English quickly fell back to the river but were unable to cross over, and there on the west bank of the Pawtucket, cut off from all retreat, Peirce fought and fell. All but eight of his Plymouth soldiers and a few friendly Indians were either killed or captured.

The survivors made their way back to Rehoboth with the tragic news, and two days later that town was attacked by the Indian victors. Since most of the inhabitants had already fled, and the few who remained were in a garrison house, the Narragansetts reduced Rehoboth to a shambles without any opposition. And on the following day they swooped upon Providence.

The Indians' long-time friend, Roger Williams, was there, but most of the people had taken refuge, along with those of Rehoboth, on Aquidneck Island. With characteristic fearlessness and calm demeanor, the aging patriarch made a futile plea for peace. He warned Canonchet that he was engaged in a losing fight. Massachusetts could raise thousands of men, Williams said, and that failing, England would send over an army large enough to exterminate all the Indians in New England. The Narragansett sachem scorned both the proposal for peace and the warning. He promised, though, that no harm would come to Roger Williams or to any member of his family, and the promise was kept. But most of the houses in Providence were plundered and burned.

His victories had given Canonchet a false feeling of

security. Thinking that the Narragansett country had
been swept clean of both settlers and soldiers and that
they would not soon return, he went into his home
territory, early in April, with only thirty of his men
to obtain from hidden caches the seed corn that the
Indians badly needed for planting in the fields along
the Connecticut River. He did not even send out any
scouts. Thus he was unaware that a company of some
fifty Connecticut soldiers, and a number of Pequots
and Mohegans, under Captain George Denison were
ranging over the country. Nor did he know that while
he was searching for the seed corn the English had by
chance come upon two stray Indians with their squaws.
The men were promptly killed and the squaws were
taken captive.

Luck in generous measure was with the English soldiers that day. The old squaws knew the whereabouts
of Canonchet, and concerned only with saving their
own skins, pointed the way. Over yonder at the foot
of a hill the sachem could be found in a hut, they told
the Englishmen.

It was a pathetic touch of irony that at this hour of
his doom, Canonchet sat dressed in a coat frilled with
silver lace that had been a gift from the colonists when
they were trying to persuade him not to become King
Philip's ally. Over this he had thrown a red blanket.
He sat there at ease, with his long, sinewy brown legs
stretched out, talking to a small group of his warriors.

Sentinels had been posted on the crest of the hill,
but the first word Canonchet had of danger was when

they burst into the hut shouting, "The English are coming!"

With one tremendous leap, the great warrior was outside the shelter, fleeing for his life. Sighting him at once, the soldiers and their Indian allies took up the chase. For some distance they ran at top speed, the hunters and the hunted. With the powerful strides of an athlete, the tall sachem reached the river and then raced desperately along the bank, looking for a shallow place to cross. Along the way he had pulled free of his coat and now, naked and unencumbered except for his gun, which he had snatched up, he was rapidly outdistancing all his pursuers except one.

That was a Pequot who also ran with the easy, loping gait of the swift Indian runner, and he was not far behind when Canonchet suddenly plunged into the river along a narrow, shallow stretch and started across. He had almost reached the opposite shore when his foot struck a stone and he stumbled and fell, wetting his gun.

The Pequot was upon him as he struggled out of the water, but there was no fight left in the warrior-chieftain. Stoically, he accepted the fate that had overtaken him, and surrendered to his captor without resistance.

Robert Staunton, twenty-one years of age, was the first Englishman to reach Canonchet's side. The young man eagerly questioned the renowned captive about his conquests. The sachem listened to him patiently and courteously. Then he said, "You are too much of a child—you do not understand matters of war. Let your chief come—him I will answer."

Canonchet was led to Stonington, Connecticut, and once more he stood before white authorities. Once more he was offered a reward if he would refuse to aid King Philip and would surrender all the Wampanoags in his territory. This time he came in chains, and the reward offered him was not a fancy, frilled coat and a belt of wampum, but his life.

There was the cutting edge of anger and scorn in his voice when he replied: "Let me hear no more of this. I will not surrender a Wampanoag nor the paring of a Wampanoag's nail."

When told that he would be shot, the chieftain's only comment was: "I like it well. I shall die before my heart is soft, or before I have said anything unworthy of myself."

The sentence of execution was carried out by the Pequots. They brought the Narragansett sachem down with a hail of bullets, and then the Mohegans took over the grisly business of cutting off his head, and quartering and burning his body.

The War Council at Hartford, Connecticut, duly acknowledged receipt of Canonchet's head, and the people who flocked to see it happily declared it to be the greatest trophy that had thus far fallen into the hands of the English, as indeed it was.

Of all the tribal leaders, Canonchet came closest in stature to King Philip. He had Philip's manly dignity and pride, and like him was a relentless foe of the Eng-

lish. And as a warrior-sachem the Narragansett probably surpassed Philip in courage. For it was known that
he had fought in the Great Swamp Fight and had led
his warriors in assaults upon the colonial troops,
whereas there was no evidence that the Wampanoag
sachem ever took part in any of the fighting.

Canonchet's death was a stunning blow to the Indian cause, but the terror and the loss of brave soldiers
and defenseless settlers were not yet over. The enemy
continued to strike boldly and successfully at various
places, and there was the horrifying slaughter at Green
Hill. Preceding this massacre, Sudbury was attacked
by approximately 500 Indians. Situated on the east
bank of the Sudbury River, it was an important town,
for roads radiated from it to settlements to the east,
the south, and the west.

On the night of April 20, the Indians came over
from Mount Wachusett and hid in the woods around
Sudbury. Instead of the dawn's early light on the
morning of the twenty-first, the people who had spent
the night in the garrisons looked out upon a conflagra-
tion. The enemy had crept in and had promptly set
fire to the unoccupied dwellings, and the flames were
now leaping skyward.

News of the attack on Sudbury soon reached Boston,
Watertown, and Concord. And the first outside help
came from a rashly brave handful of armed men who
hurried down from Concord. They were slain by the
Indians who lay concealed in the tall grass of Sudbury's river meadow.

Captain Edward Cowell, returning to Boston with eighteen troopers, was attacked a short distance from Sudbury, and four of his men were killed. The rest of the force reached the town, and soon afterward Captain Hugh Mason and his company marched in safely from Watertown, and with Cowell's troopers succeeded in driving the enemy back to the western side of the river. But the ominous sound of firing from the west could be heard. When Captain Mason led the troops across the river to give the assistance that seemed to be needed, he was compelled to retreat. It was well that he did, for otherwise the losses suffered by the English that day would probably have been heavier.

At the garrison in Marlborough, across the river to the southwest, Captain Samuel Wadsworth had learned about the assault. Accompanied by Captain Samuel Brocklebank, he had marched off with between fifty and sixty men to the relief of Sudbury. About a mile from the town he glimpsed a number of warriors on the path ahead and saw them run into the woods. It was as if sight of the Indians triggered an irresistible impulse to follow them. Experienced soldier though he was, and with the lessons of so many fatal ambushes to deter him, Captain Wadsworth threw caution to the winds and followed the retreating enemy.

He had not gone far when there was a sudden explosion of musket fire and the wild yelping of several hundred warriors. The English soldiers fought their way to the top of an elevation nearby named Green Hill. And there, protected by trees and rocks, they kept up a heroic fight for their lives throughout the afternoon.

Toward sunset the Indians resorted to their favorite weapon. They set fire to the brush and the grass around the hill. Choked and almost blinded by smoke, the exhausted troops were forced to leave their shelters, and make a frantic effort to escape by fleeing from the hill. Fourteen of the men succeeded. The rest were quickly gunned down by the foe. As dusk fell, the Indians retreated, leaving the stripped bodies of Wadsworth and Brocklebank, and some thirty or more of their men, strewn about Green Hill.

Saddened and depressed as New Englanders were by their losses in the Battle of Green Hill, they were soon rejoicing over the recovery of some of the English settlers who had been held captive by the Indians. The Bay Colony had begun negotiations with the enemy around Mount Wachusett in April, proposing either the exchange of English for Indian prisoners or the return of the former for payment of a ransom. Two Christian Indians, Tom Dublet and Peter Conway, had represented the government at two conferences with the sachems, but without satisfactory results. On a third trip they were accompanied by John Hoar, a citizen of Concord, and on May 2, Hoar was able to obtain the release of Mrs. Mary Rowlandson by paying a ransom of £20.

Before the end of June more than twenty other

Indian prisoners had either been ransomed or had escaped, and among the former were the son and daughter of the Rowlandsons. The journal that Mary Rowlandson subsequently wrote, and which has been preserved, relates in vivid and harrowing detail the experiences of this intrepid woman as an Indian captive.

10 *White Woman Captive*

In the afternoon of February 10, 1676, the victorious Indians left Lancaster, marching westward with their white captives. About a mile from the town they halted to camp for the night on top of a hill from which the unfortunate prisoners could look back upon the smoking ruins of what had so recently been their comfortable homes.

Now, shivering with cold and terror, they watched

their captors make gleeful preparations for a night of feasting and wild celebration. The Indians had driven off horses, cattle, sheep, and pigs from the plundered town, and they soon had slaughtered animals roasting over the fires they had built and around which they capered in exultant abandon. "This was the dolefulest night that my eyes ever saw," Mrs. Rowlandson reported. "Oh, the roaring and singing, the dancing and yelling, of those black creatures, which made the place a lively resemblance of hell."

Having gorged themselves with food, and with characteristic wastefulness left behind enough to have lived on for many days, the Indians marched again the next morning into the "vast and desolate wilderness." In the stinging cold, the miserable captives struggled along as best they could. Mrs. Rowlandson was allowed to ride a horse bareback, holding her desperately wounded little girl before her. But while going down a steep hill, both mother and child pitched forward over the horse's head and fell to the ground. No one came to help the poor woman to her feet—instead, some of her captors guffawed, and ridiculed her for not being able to stay on the horse.

It began to snow, and with darkness falling early in the winter afternoon, the Indians stopped to camp for the night in the woods. Crouched in the shelter of a few boughs beside a small fire, Mrs. Rowlandson sat on the snow-covered ground, trying vainly to comfort her suffering child. During the bitter night her own wounded side stiffened so that she could scarcely stand up when morning finally came.

Faint from suffering and from lack of food, she was grateful for the unexpected kindness shown her that day by an Indian who lifted her and her child upon his horse, and let them ride behind him when the march began again. In the afternoon captors and captives came to the Indian village of Menameset upon the banks of the Ware River to the north of Brookfield. "Oh, the number of pagans that came about me!" Mrs. Rowlandson exclaimed. There were many more than those in the company with which she had come, for numerous Indians had already assembled here to get ready for expeditions against the English settlements. Among them was an English prisoner named Robert Pepper, who had been captured the previous fourth of September in the ambush of Captain Richard Beers and his men while they were on their way to evacuate Northfield, Massachusetts. Mrs. Rowlandson and Pepper had a brief visit together, and he told her of having treated his leg wound with oak leaves. "Then I did the same," she reported, "and was cured."

Here at Menameset the pastor's wife was permitted to occupy a rude wigwam, and here she sat for five days nursing her dying child. On the eighteenth of February death came mercifully to the little girl named Sarah, and the Indians buried her on a hill.

When Mrs. Rowlandson was driven by the flames

from her home in Lancaster, a Narragansett Indian
had seized her and claimed her as his property. This
Indian sold her to the Narragansett sachem Quinnapin, and she became the maid of Weetamoo, squaw
sachem of the Pocassets, and now the wife of Quinnapin. The two older Rowlandson children, Mary and
Joseph, had each been sold to a different Indian master, and the few occasions upon which their mother saw
them were more fraught with heartache than with joy,
for they were soon separated, each pathetic captive
going his separate way in the wilderness.

For a few days the war drums beat in Menameset,
the war dances were danced, and the warriors held
powwows around the council fires. Then several hundred braves started out on the trails leading to Medfield, Massachusetts. At daybreak on the twenty-first of
February, the inhabitants of that hapless town were
awakened by yelling that seemed "to make the earth
tremble," and a few hours later Medfield, like Lancaster before it, had become a smoking, smoldering
ruin.

The triumphant warriors came trooping back to
Menameset "with outrageous roaring and whooping,"
announcing their victory long before reaching the village. And upon their arrival—"Oh, the hideous exult-
ing there was over some English scalps they had taken
and brought back with them," Mrs. Rowlandson shud-
deringly related. But in the midst of the horror of
looking upon the bloody scalps of her countrymen, she
saw, too, evidence of the "wonderful mercy of God."

For in the plunder that one of the Medfield attackers had brought back there was a Bible, and the Indian gave the precious book to Mary Rowlandson. Henceforth, in the darkest hours of her captivity, she took this cherished Bible from the deep pocket in her skirt and found solace and strength from reading the Scriptures.

Suddenly there was bedlam in the village as the Indians made hasty preparations for departure. Their scouts had brought intelligence that an English force was marching to attack them. One wretched prisoner did not live to march again with her captors. Lacking the stamina of the pastor's wife, poor Mrs. Joslin could not control her weeping, so the Indians killed her, and her small child, after an hour of ceremonious singing and dancing.

For their own sick and decrepit members, the Indians showed the greatest solicitude. Husky warriors carried their weak old mothers on their backs. Younger women, already burdened by papooses strapped to their backs, lifted tired children and carried them in their arms. One heavy sick Indian was borne on a litter by four of his strong companions.

Cold, wet, hungry, and weary, Mrs. Rowlandson staggered on for miles with the retreating Indians. Several days after leaving Menameset they came on a Friday to Miller's River. At once the men went to work cutting down trees and building rafts. Food had become so scarce that there was little to eat except parched meal. But for supper on Saturday there was broth made by boiling an old horse's leg in a big kettle, which was filled up with water again whenever it was emptied. Mrs. Rowlandson was so starved that she gulped down the horse broth, and found it delicious.

The pastor's wife was now at the beck and call of her mistress, and during the intervals when the Indians rested in camp, she was often busy knitting stockings for the squaw sachem. When Weetamoo ordered her to work at her knitting on the following day, Mrs. Rowlandson pleaded to be allowed to keep the Sabbath holy, promising to double her efforts on Monday. But she was sternly warned that her face would be smashed if she did not do as she was ordered.

Meanwhile the Indians had begun crossing the river on their rafts. There were hundreds of them—old and young, some sick and some lame, and many squaws with papooses on their backs. It was not until Monday that all of them reached the northern shore. Knowing that the English soldiers were approaching, Mrs. Rowlandson looked back with agonizing heartache. It was, in fact, little more than the width of the river that separated her from them and rescue, for Major Thomas Savage reached its banks on the south side shortly after the Indians had crossed over, and decided to give up the chase.

Marching in a northwesterly direction toward the Connecticut River, the Indians forded icy brooks and hurried on with all possible speed. Mrs. Rowlandson stumbled along "mourning and lamenting," for in leaving her own country farther and farther behind, she felt as if she were being swallowed up by the "vast and howling wilderness." After spending a night near a great swamp, the Indians pushed on and came to the abandoned town of Northfield (or, by its Indian name, Squakeag). Here they stopped and spread out over the deserted fields like swarms of hungry locusts, gleaning corn and some wheat they found frozen in the shocks.

The next morning they moved on up the Connecticut River a few miles to a point at which they crossed over in canoes to a rendezvous on the west bank with Philip and a large party of warriors already gathered there. "Then my heart began to fail," Mrs. Rowlandson said, "and I fell aweeping, which was the first time I had wept before the Indians." But there was one who assured her that she would not be killed, and another who tried to comfort her by giving her a half pint of peas.

The council fires burned brightly again; the warriors beat their drums and shouted vengeance on the white enemy; and the squaws shuffled around boiling groundnuts and parching corn—provisions for the Indians who were getting ready to raid the Connecticut Valley towns.

After their departure, Mrs. Rowlandson was taken to the wigwam of the Wampanoag sachem. Philip received her with courtesy, invited her to sit upon a mat beside him, and offered her a pipe to smoke, which the pastor's wife declined. He asked her to make a shirt for his young son, which she willingly agreed to do,

and when the work was finished he gave her a shil-
ling. With such unexpected riches, Mrs. Rowlandson
bought a hunk of horse meat. There was a day, too,
when she also made a cap for the boy, and Philip
invited her to share with him a meal of pancakes made
of parched wheat, beaten and fried in bear's grease.

Another order for a boy's shirt came from a squaw
who gave Mrs. Rowlandson a slab of bear's meat for
doing the work; and for knitting a pair of stockings for
a second Indian woman, she received a quart of peas.
The boiled dinner of peas and bear was a feast such
as the half-famished woman seldom had to satisfy the
pangs of hunger.

The raiders returned from the valley towns bringing horses and sheep, and after they had gorged and
celebrated for a few days, they broke up into various
groups, and departed. Those who remained took Mrs.
Rowlandson and several other captives six miles farther up the river, and then crossed to the eastern bank.
Weetamoo, Quinnapin, and Philip had all gone elsewhere, and the sufferings and privations that the pastor's wife now had to endure were almost too great
even for her stout heart and strong spirit.

One bitter cold day the Indians were huddled
around the fires in their wigwams, but Mrs. Rowlandson went from one to another without being allowed
to creep anywhere near the fire. Almost perishing with
cold, she came timidly to yet one more smoky wigwam,
and among the Indians there was a squaw who made
room for her, laid a mat for her to sit on, and slipped

a handful of groundnuts into her pocket. She would be welcome to come again when she was cold and hungry, the squaw told her.

Gnawing hunger soon drove the poor woman back to this kind squaw to beg for a little food. But the Indian in whose custody she had been left came looking for her, and finding her in the wigwam, ordered her out and kicked her all the way back. That night the Indians roasted a deer, but they did not offer Mrs. Rowlandson even a taste of the savory venison. "Sometimes I met with favor," she said, "and sometimes with nothing but frowns."

The next day the seemingly aimless wandering commenced again. Uncomplaining, the pastor's wife took up her load and marched off again with her captors. Wading streams and climbing steep hills, her head became so light she feared that she was going to faint. Finally, on the following day, she did protest that the skin had been rubbed off her back, but she was told that it would not matter if her head were off, too.

Some distance down the Connecticut River the Indians came to a "mighty thicket of brush" where they stopped to rest. Here Mrs. Rowlandson made a little shirt for a papoose and was given a "mess of broth thickened with meal made from the bark of a tree." Some warriors soon came yelping into the covert, bringing a white captive and reporting that they had killed three Englishmen at Hadley. The prisoner was Thomas Read, who gave Mrs. Rowlandson the heartening news that he had recently seen her husband in

Boston and that he was well but very melancholy. She
had been told by her captors that her husband had
been killed.

At the end of a fortnight in the thicket, the Indians
packed up and were off again. But now, with some
groundnuts in her pocket and a load on her back, Mrs.
Rowlandson went along cheerfully, having her burden
more on her back than on her spirit, she said, for she
was buoyed up by the hope of going home to her
husband.

That happy prospect came closer to realization soon
afterward when an Indian messenger appeared in the
camp with an order from Quinnapin that Mrs. Rowlandson should be taken to Mount Wachusett, where
representatives of the English were conferring with
the sachems about redeeming her and other captives.
"My heart was now so light that I could run," the
pastor's wife related. "My strength seemed to come
again, and to recruit my feeble knees and aching
heart."

There were more weary, hungry days of marching,
but at last the Indians reached Mount Wachusett. Negotiations for the release of their captives were still
going on, and Mrs. Rowlandson saw and talked to the
Praying Indians Tom Dublet and Peter Conway, who
were there representing the authorities in Boston. She
was still waiting for the moment when she would be
free to return to her own people when a large body
of warriors left Mount Wachusett for the attack on

Sudbury, Massachusetts, which they launched at daybreak on April 21.

It was a great victory for the Indians. "Yet," Mrs.
Rowlandson reported, "they came home without the
rejoicing over their victory which they were wont to
show at other times. Rather, they were like dogs which
have lost their ears." They had begun to realize, with
sobering effect, that they were becoming weaker day
by day, while the English were growing stronger.

But there was one more celebration of Indian victories that Mrs. Rowlandson saw near the end of her
captivity. It was a dance at which Quinnapin and
Weetamoo were conspicuous performers. The squaw
sachem was resplendent in a shaggy horseman's coat
lavishly ornamented with wampum. From the wrists
to the elbows, her arms were encircled with bracelets,
and necklaces hung over her well-rounded shoulders.
There were flashing jewels in her ears, too, and she
wore red stockings and white shoes. Her face was
painted a brilliant crimson, and her black hair was
powdered white. This was the last time that Mrs. Rowlandson saw the "severe and proud dame" for whom
she had worked as a slave.

Soon after the dance, King Philip, who was there
with his warriors, sent for Mrs. Rowlandson, and
asked, "What would you give me to tell you some good
news?" To which she replied that she would give him
anything she had, but what did he want?

"Two coats, twenty shillings, half a bushel of seed

corn, and some tobacco," Philip replied, perhaps in jest.

"I thanked him," Mrs. Rowlandson related, "but I knew the good news as well as the crafty fox did." For the last time she had seen and spoken to the Wampanoag sachem.

About sundown the next day, Mrs. Rowlandson, accompanied by John Hoar and the two Praying Indians, came to Lancaster. "It was a solemn sight to me," she said. "There I had lived many comfortable years among my relatives and neighbors, and now there was not one Christian to be seen—not one house left standing."

The pastor's wife and her escort spent the night in an abandoned farmhouse on the outskirts of the town, having found some straw to sleep on. Before noon the next day of May 3, they passed through Concord, and, hurrying on, arrived that afternoon in Boston. After three months of Indian captivity, brave Mary Rowlandson was joyfully reunited with her husband.

11 The Turning Point of the War

Toward the end of April, Indian raids had begun to fall off both in number and in violence. Hunger had become an enemy that stalked the tribes, whose strength had been greatly reduced by the ravages of disease and by heavy losses in their war with the English. All through the winter food had been so scarce that at times the Indians had been close to starvation. And now with their supplies exhausted, replenishment had become a necessity. So they began to move back in large numbers to their old fishing grounds at the falls of the rivers.

The main concentration of hungry tribes was at Peskeompscut on the Connecticut River about five miles above Deerfield. Here they erected their wig-wams in three villages—on opposite banks of the river at the head of the falls, and the third on an island some distance below. Besides the fishing grounds, there were the cleared fields around abandoned Deerfield, where the Indians hoped to raise a crop with the seed corn they had managed to save. While the women, children, and old men fished and planted, the warriors raided the settlers' cattle in the lower valley towns.

Having learned that the English had turned out a herd to graze in the meadows of Hatfield, a raiding party pushed rapidly down the valley on the night of May 12 and drove off seventy head of cattle. The marauders were well along the trail on the way back to their villages with the stolen cows before the en-raged farmers discovered their losses. They were clam-oring to strike back at the Indians when a young man appeared unexpectedly in Hatfield. John Gilbert had escaped from his captors at Peskeompscut after having been captured by the enemy near Springfield early in April.

This was a kind of windfall for the settlers since Gilbert could give them firsthand information about the Indians' encampment at the falls. He assured them that a successful attack would not be too difficult, as the warriors felt so secure they had grown careless about taking measures to protect the villages against surprise.

There was no strong military force in the valley at this time. So Captain William Turner, in command of the garrison troops, hesitated to march against the Indians. But it was an opportunity to strike a blow that might never come again. With the planting over and the fish dried, the enemy would soon be on the move and on the warpath once more. Volunteers from Hatfield, Northampton, and Hadley were not lacking, and the decision to undertake the extremely risky venture was made.

Able-bodied men, boys, and garrison soldiers, numbering about 180, gathered in Hatfield on the eighteenth of May. Soon after sunset they filed out the gates of the stockade and took the trail leading north to Deerfield. They reached its fire-blackened ruins at midnight and pushed on across the Green River. And beyond the great white ash swamp to the east, they came to high ground just before daybreak.

Dismounting and leaving their horses picketed here, they forded shallow Fall River near the point at which it converged with the Connecticut River. The Indian village stood on the north bank of the river, and the attacking force stole in among the unguarded wigwams. The Indians were probably sleeping all the more soundly for having gorged on English beef the previous day.

Some of them never awakened. They were killed in

their sleep by the blasts of musketry as the English fired directly into the wigwams. Others tried to escape in canoes, but many of them were dashed to their deaths on the rocks below the falls. After the carnage in the village was over, the wigwams were fired, stores of dried fish were destroyed, and two forges used by the Indians for repairing their muskets were demolished.

But in the excitement of wreaking vengeance upon the foe, Turner and his men had forgotten about the other Indian camps. They discovered too late that warrior parties, alerted by sounds of the fierce assault, were swarming in from the other side of the river and from the island below. It was now the English who fled in panic, making a wild dash for their mounts tethered in the woods nearby. But the Indians were there first, and many of the horses were not recovered by the attacking force.

In the disorganized retreat, groups of men, some mounted and others on foot, fought desperately to shake free of the Indians pressing hard on their flanks. While crossing Green River, Captain Turner was shot through the back and fell dead at the river's edge. That the rout did not end in wholesale massacre was owing to the courageous leadership of Samuel Holyoke, Turner's second-in-command. Flight and pursuit continued until the broken company reached Deerfield, where the Indians gave up the chase and turned back. Later in the day the exhausted men arrived in Hatfield, and during the next three or four days, lone survivors who had become separated from the others came limping in.

The audacious venture had taken a heavy toll of Turner's small force—more than forty of the men were killed. But the English had dealt the enemy a severe blow. By a rough estimate, several hundred Indians, including women and children, had lost their lives.

The fallen warriors could not be replaced, and it was becoming more and more difficult to obtain arms and ammunition. Just as serious was the failure of the Indians' plan to lay in stores of dried fish at the falls, and to reap their crops in the abandoned fields while they terrorized the valley settlers and drove off their livestock. Successful plundering of the English towns was no longer so easy as it had been, for the settlements were now palisaded and garrisoned by soldiers alert to the enemy's tactics.

In contrast to the depleted resources of their foe, the English were not limited either in manpower or in the material resources necessary to wage war. And their commanders, who had been so inept in the earlier stages of the conflict, were beginning to grasp and apply the principles of forest warfare. They were making increasing use, too, of the invaluable services of friendly Indians. Aware of the weaknesses of the enemy Indians on the one hand and of their own growing strength on the other, the English felt an upsurge of confidence in their ability to win the war.

Immediately after the action at the rapids (now

Turners Falls), the towns in the upper valley were strengthened by additional troops. And within a few weeks, Connecticut and Massachusetts each raised a large, well-equipped force. Under the respective commands of Major John Talcott and Captain Daniel Henchman, the combined armies of almost a thousand men marched up to the falls to make an assault upon the remaining Indians. All that the expedition accomplished was the discovery that the villages were deserted, the former inhabitants having departed for refuge in places unknown to the English.

In the meantime, enemy activity had shifted to Plymouth. Groups of Indians had made forays on several towns, including Taunton and Bridgewater. Plans were made to organize a small force for patrol duty along the frontier. And Benjamin Church seemed to be the right man to lead such a company, so the government sent him a message, requesting that he come to Plymouth.

Ever since the attack upon the Narragansetts in the Great Swamp Fight, Church had been inactive. The wound he had suffered in that engagement had left him with a stiff leg. For several months he had been convalescing on Aquidneck Island at the home of his old friend Captain John Almy. Here, in the company of his family and friends, he waited impatiently for news of the war's progress, and became increasingly restless from forced inactivity.

Church would test the bad leg, moving it cautiously, and then shake his head. "No, too stiff and too sore," he would say. "I couldn't even mount a horse. And as for running through those bogs, I'd fall at the first try, and presently find myself without my scalp." Fortunately, he gradually regained full use of the leg, and when the summons came from Plymouth he set off eagerly to see what the government had to offer him.

At the first conference, Church's enthusiasm quickly turned to disappointment. The authorities proposed that he take command of a company of sixty or seventy men to patrol some of the outlying towns where it was feared the Indians would strike soon again.

Impatiently Church spoke his mind. "If I take command of a company," he said, "I will not lie in any town or garrison house waiting for the enemy to come. I will hunt them in the woods and fight them the way they fight us. What can you expect these small companies to gain when our foe lies in ambush by the hundreds in every swamp and alongside every wooded pass? Does it mean nothing to you that the valiant Captain Wadsworth and his company were destroyed and many others I could name? Where will we be if many more of our finest officers are killed?"

Church answered his own question as he sat down, "In the scalping hands of the enemy, gentlemen."

"What would you suggest, Mr. Church?" a member of the War Council inquired.

Church was instantly on his feet. "Raise 300 soldiers at once," he urged. "If we want to make an end to this war, we must fight with everything we have, as our foes are doing."

Then Church squared his shoulders and told the council what he would do if they would cooperate. Give him 200 seasoned soldiers and 100 friendly Indians for a six-week march in the woods, and he had no doubt but what he could give them good service.

The members of the War Council shook their heads, and hedged. They were already heavily in debt, they said, and as for sending out the Indians—well, would it be advisable to trust that many on a scouting expedition in the woods? In unconcealed disgust, Church picked up his hat and returned to Aquidneck Island.

But he was not comfortable after he had cooled off, and on Tuesday, June 8, he was back in Plymouth. The General Court was in session, and to Church's surprise they welcomed him warmly and told him how glad they were to see him alive. Smiling, he remarked, "And I am glad to see *you* alive. I have seen so many fires and smokes over here on your side of the country since I left that I have not been able to eat or sleep with any comfort for fear you had all been destroyed."

The authorities had reconsidered Church's proposals, and they were now ready, they told him, to raise the quota he had urged and to enlist the services of the friendly Indians. Church did not tarry long. Having been given permission to recruit some of the Plymouth Colony refugees on Aquidneck Island, he hastened southward to Falmouth. Here he hired two Indians to paddle him in a canoe over to the island.

As they neared Sakonnet Point, Church caught sight

of some Indians fishing from the rocks along the shore. Since the beginning of the war, he had wanted to talk with the Sakonnet Indians again, for he believed he could draw them away from Philip. Here was the opportunity. So he directed his oarsmen to paddle over to the rocky point.

After a wary approach, and friendly signs from the Sakonnet fishermen, Church clambered up the rocks to meet them. It was a pleasant surprise to find George there. He was one of the Sakonnets who had brought him the invitation to Awashonks' dance. Church's first question, of course, was to ask about the squaw sachem.

"She is in a swamp about three miles from here," George answered in his good English. "She does not like this war with the white men. She has left Philip, and she says she will not go back to him."

Church was not ready for the meeting with the squaw sachem that George wanted to arrange then and there, but he promised to come back in a few days to a place they agreed upon.

Awashonks did not disappoint Church when he returned to see her. Painted and adorned for the occasion in necklaces and bracelets, she came down to the shore with her retinue. All of them greeted Church with friendly handshakes. But he was suddenly dismayed to see a band of hostile Indians rise up from the tall grass and surround them. Betraying no sign of surprise or alarm, he protested to the squaw sachem that it was not customary to come heavily armed for a peace talk. With conspicuous lack of good grace, the braves laid aside their guns after Awashonks had spoken to them in their own tongue.

The foresighted Mr. Church had brought a bottle of rum and tobacco. Now he pulled out his calabash and, pouring some rum into the gourd, drank to the squaw sachem's health, noticing how closely she watched to see if he swallowed the liquor.

When offered a drink, she shook her head and said, "You—you drink again." This time Church laughed, poured rum into his cupped palm, downed it, and said, "See! There's no poison in that."

Convinced now that she would not drop dead if she drank the rum, Awashonks took a hearty swallow and passed the rest to her attendants. Then Church distributed the tobacco, and everybody was suddenly in the mood to talk.

Awashonks reproached Church for not having come back to see her as he had promised. "If you had," she said, "we might never have joined Philip against the English."

Church explained that the sudden outbreak of hostilities had prevented him from returning soon after his visit with her at the war dance. "And when I did make the attempt," he said, "I was set upon by a band of Indians at Punkatees and had to fight a whole afternoon to save my little company of nineteen men." It was the Battle of the Peas Field that he recalled.

A murmurous hubbub arose among Awashonks' fierce-looking warriors. One of them threatened

Church with his sword, but other Indians grabbed the surly fellow. The interpreter explained. "He says, Mr. Church, that you killed his brother at Punkatees and therefore he thirsts for your blood."

"Tell him," Church replied heatedly, "that if his brother had stayed at Sakonnet, where I urged him to remain, he would not have been killed."

Awashonks' chief captain stood up and commanded silence. "Let us talk no more about old things," he counseled. With that the turbulence subsided and they sat down to discuss peace.

Benjamin Church pleaded eloquently with Awashonks and her warriors to break their ties with Philip and to come over to the side of the English. "It is not in my power to conclude a peace treaty with you," he told them honestly, "but I will speak to the governor in your behalf."

At last, after much talk and debate, Church persuaded the Sakonnets to give themselves up to the English, and to serve them as allies against Philip on the condition that the Plymouth Government spare their lives and promise not to transport them out of the country. Then Church expressed his pleasure over their being reunited in friendship with the English.

The chief captain rose and said, "Sir, if you will please accept me and my men and will lead us, we will fight for you, and we will help you get Philip's head before the Indian corn is ripe."

12 Celebration of Peace with the Sakonnets

Before the Indian corn is ripe! The words exhilarated Benjamin Church, and charged his whole being with a driving energy. Just one purpose dominated him now. He was determined that before the Indian corn was ripe he would have King Philip's head. There was much to be done. Before he plunged into the woods to track down Philip, he had to keep faith with the Sakonnets. He had to have the Plymouth Government's assurance that they would be treated honorably.

At the conclusion of the peace meeting with Awashonks and her people, Church had been impatient to depart at once for Plymouth by the shorter way through the woods. But the Indians had dissuaded him because of the danger of skulking enemy warriors, who were only too eager to have *his* head. So he planned instead to go part of the way by boat, and instructed the five Indians who had been chosen to accompany him to Plymouth to meet him at Sakonnet Point, where he would pick them up.

When Church approached the Point on the day agreed upon, the Indians were there on the rocks waiting for him. But the weather was foul, the water was choppy, and the canoe the Sakonnets had brought was broken. So only Peter, Awashonks' son, hazarded the crossing and got safely aboard Church's boat. Then it began to rain and blow so hard that they had to make for the southern shore of Aquidneck Island. Church changed his plans again. He went ashore at Newport, wrote an account of his visit with Awashonks, and drew up a draft of proposals and articles of peace.

Peter returned to Sakonnet Point, and shortly afterward headed for Plymouth on foot, accompanied by some of Awashonks' men, to deliver the sealed document to the authorities there.

In the meantime the Plymouth Government had ordered out a new expedition, and Major William Bradford, in command of the army, was now in Pocasset country. After dispatching Peter on his mission, Church came to give the major a full report on his dealings with the Sakonnets, and to recommend that he accept their surrender.

Following Bradford's orders, Church went back to Sakonnet Point and explained to Awashonks that she must bring all her people to the English camp in Pocasset. On the last day of June, the squaw sachem arrived there, and appeared before the major with about one hundred Sakonnets. Church was present, and at once asked for the release of the warriors to serve under him in the field. But Bradford brusquely informed him that he could not take responsibility for the Indians, and ordered all the Sakonnets to proceed to Sandwich, a town situated on Cape Cod between Plymouth and Barnstable.

The squaw sachem and her chief men clustered around Church in alarm, but he reassured them, and advised them to obey Major Bradford's orders. He promised to come to Sandwich himself as soon as he could bring a report on the peace proposals from the governor. So, confident that Mr. Church would take care of her people, Awashonks led them off eastward behind a flag of truce.

Church remained for a while with the army that now began an intensive search for enemy Indians. A captured Pocasset named Toby had informed Major Bradford that a large number of them were digging for clams at Waypoiset near the mouth of the Kicka-muit River—Pocassets, Wampanoags, and Narragansetts, he said. And he added that Philip himself was expected there within three or four days.

The English troops embarked on Rhode Island boats, and as they came near the northern tip of Aquidneck Island at dusk, they could see the Indians' fires at Waypoiset. Church refrained with difficulty from giving the order himself to hasten on and take the clam diggers by surprise. And he snorted when he heard Bradford direct the boats westward for a landing on Mount Hope Peninsula.

No reason was given for this maneuver, and nothing came of it. It has been surmised that Major Bradford may have planned to intercept Philip on his way down to join the Indians at their clamming place. The army advanced up Mount Hope Peninsula to Rehoboth, and here it was strengthened by a body of troopers under Captain Thomas Brattle, and a company of foot soldiers commanded by Captain Moseley.

Connecticut soldiers had been active, too, scouring the Narragansett country. In the last week of June, Captain Talcott had reorganized his army at Norwich, and with a large force of English troopers and Indian allies, took up the hunt again. On the morning of July 2, his scouts discovered an enemy encampment in a cedar swamp on the south bank of the Pawtuxet River. Talcott closed in on it, and as the mounted soldiers circled the swamp, the Mohegans and Pequots rushed in and flushed out the startled Narragansetts. Their resistance was so feeble that they were soon overpowered. In this attack 171 Indians, including women

and children, were killed or captured. Among the
slain, Talcott reported, was "that old piece of venom,
saunk squaw Quaiapin."

The power of the once proud and mighty Narragansetts had been completely broken, most of them
having been killed, captured, or driven out of their
territory. There was no spirit left in the few who remained. A group of about eighty came forlornly into
Warwick to wait for the return of their leader, who
was trying to find out from the authorities in Providence how his people could get safely to Boston to
make peace with the Massachusetts Government. Talcott found them there in Warwick, and ruthlessly
killed or captured all but a handful.

Disillusioned with Philip's cause, and weary of the
hopeless contest, more and more of the Wampanoag
sachem's former allies were trying to save their lives
by giving themselves up to the colonial governments.
Many took advantage of the offer made by Massachusetts and Plymouth in a proclamation that promised
mercy to those Indians who surrendered within a
stated period of time.

Early in July, Sagamore Sam, speaking for himself
and other frightened Nipmuck leaders, made an abject
appeal in a letter to the governor of Massachusetts,
which read in part: "Mr. John Leverett, my Lord, and
all the chief men: We beseech you all to help us. My
wife she is but one, but there be more prisoners which
we pray you keep well. And that further you will consider about the making of peace. We would agree with

you and make a Covenant of Peace with you. We have been destroyed by your soldiers, but still we remember it now to sit still."

To fight no more but to "sit still" and plead for leniency from the stronger race that had virtually conquered their tribes now seemed the only course left to most of the sachems and sagamores. Their pleading, like that of Sagamore Sam's, fell on deaf ears, though. The English declared that there would be no mercy for the chief men who had drawn their people into the war and who were themselves guilty of unforgivable atrocities. Mercy, they said, would be extended only to those of their followers who had been forced to fight and who had not committed heinous acts of brutality.

Meanwhile, Benjamin Church had taken leave of Bradford's army, and on the morning of July 6 had arrived in Plymouth, where he was warmly greeted by Governor Josiah Winslow and Thomas Southworth, the colony treasurer. Both men listened with interest to his account of the army's activities. Then Church, in turn, heard the good news that the faithful Peter had arrived safely in Plymouth with the peace proposals and that the governor had approved them. Church informed Winslow that he would depart that afternoon to seek out the Sakonnets, for he knew how eager they were to learn what had happened since he had last seen them trudging off to Sandwich. Before he left, the governor smilingly told him that upon his return he would find a commission awaiting him and the soldiers to make up the company he desired.

It was a jubilant Church who, with a few companions, hastened down the coast to Sandwich. But there were no Indians in sight, and since it was late, the party had to spend the night there. The next day Church found the Sakonnets over to the west on the shore of Buzzards Bay, where they were having a merry time on the sands and flats. Far away from King Philip, whom they never had loved, and feeling safe under the protecting wing of Mr. Church, they were shouting and frolicking like happy children. Some were running races. There was a group kicking a ball in a lusty game of football. And others were fishing and digging for clams along the beach.

Church sent word of his arrival to Awashonks, and he was promptly escorted to a shelter, open on one side, where the squaw sachem and her chief men soon joined him. After they had heard the cheering news that Governor Winslow had approved the peace treaty, Awashonks called all her people together. There before the open shelter, the Sakonnets gathered and gave Mr. Church such salvos of applause as "made the heavens ring."

The big celebration came that evening. Toward dusk the tall, husky Sakonnets came in from the woods loaded with dry pine tops and boughs. They were piled in one great heap on the sand in front of the shelter. Meanwhile, the squaws had been busy over their fires cooking huge platters of fish.

With supper over, the towering pile of pine knots

and branches was lighted, and as the flames leaped high, all the Indians—little children and big braves—gathered in circles around the bonfire. In the first ring nearest the fire, Awashonks knelt with her oldest men and women. Behind them stood the warriors. In the outside circle, the children and other members of the tribe mingled.

The ceremony began when the chief captain stepped into the space between the fire and the first ring of spectators. Holding a long spear in one hand and a hatchet in the other, he danced around the great pine blaze, pantomiming battle with all the tribal enemies of the English. One by one he named them, and each time he plucked from the blaze a firebrand that symbolized the tribe that fought with Philip.

When all the hostile tribes had been named and fought in mock battle, the chief captain stuck his spear and hatchet in the sand, and a Sakonnet sagamore leaped forward to grasp the weapons and repeat the ritual. After six sagamores had acted out this ceremonial warfare, the captain walked over to where the guest of honor sat in front of the shelter and addressed him: "Mr. Church, we have been making soldiers for you. In this way each sagamore has sworn that he will fight for you."

The stately Awashonks now rose and spoke. "We are all ready to fight for the English," she said. "Call forth any of my warriors that you want, Mr. Church, and they will go with you to make war upon the enemy." Church thanked the squaw sachem, and promptly selected some of her stalwart men to serve under him.

Having departed at an early hour, they arrived in Plymouth later the following day. The next morning Church was handed the commission that Governor Winslow had promised he would have ready:

Captain Benjamin Church, you are hereby nominated, ordered, commissioned, and empowered to raise a company of volunteers of about two hundred men, English and Indians . . . to lead them forth now and hereafter, at such time and unto such places within this colony, or elsewhere within the federated colonies, as you should think fit; to discover, pursue, fight, surprise, destroy or subdue our Indian enemy, or any part or parties of them that, by the providence of God, you may meet with.

Benjamin Church had at last become a captain, and with a special force of English and Indian volunteers, he was ready and eager to take to the woods and track down King Philip.

13 On the Trail of the Doomed Sachem

Shortly after Church left the main army, Major Bradford marched from Rehoboth with his troops, and for some days thereafter engaged in a vigorous hunt for the enemy in the western part of Plymouth Colony. Success was easy if the Indians could be found, for they were now broken up into fugitive bands wandering hither and thither in desperate search of security, and too disheartened and too short of powder to put up much of a fight.

After his men had killed a number of them and had taken numerous prisoners, Bradford received a report that gave him high hopes of capturing Philip himself. The Wampanoag sachem was hiding in a swamp nearby, a captive Indian told the major, but his soldiers came out of it empty-handed after a sweeping search. In mid-July, Bradford established headquarters at Taunton, and his troops remained active, patrolling the area south of the Taunton River.

Meanwhile, Captain Benjamin Church had swung back into action with the dash, the vigor, and the confidence that made him the most spectacular and the most memorable of all the English leaders who fought in King Philip's War. About July 11, he marched out of Plymouth and into the woods he had known so well as a boy, heading for Middleborough with his soldiers.

They followed the old Indian trail over which Massasoit and his Wampanoag warriors had traveled to visit Plymouth when it was a weak young colony—and along which Edward Winslow and Stephen Hopkins had gone to pay a return call upon the chieftain. Those were the years when the old woodland trail linked the two races in ties of friendship. Now, some fifty-odd years later, the last of the Wampanoag sachems was being hunted like a wild animal along this and other paths that crisscrossed what had once been his father's domain.

Having left Middleborough in the gray light of early dawn, Captain Church and his company of Plymouth troops and Indians came to a swampy thicket where it was believed they would find an enemy hide-out. Indian scouts who had gone ahead returned with the report that they had seen a party of Narragansetts and Wampanoags gathered around their fires.

Church's lightning attack that followed came so unexpectedly that the Indians surrendered without a struggle. Then Church went through what was to become routine procedure whenever he captured an enemy band, large or small. With the skill of one who knew Indians and the business of fighting Indians, he questioned his prisoners with the purpose of drawing out information that might lead him to Philip's place of concealment. It was a method that paid off handsomely in quick and effective results.

Thus, it was from an Indian named Jeffrey that the captain learned of another hostile party that was assembled at Monponset Pond. With the intuition that he often displayed, Church sized up Jeffrey as an Indian who could be trusted. So he promised the prisoner that if he would be loyal, he would not be sold into slavery and shipped out of the country. Instead, he should be Church's "waiting man" who would take care of the captain's horse, and perform other personal services. Jeffrey promised and, as it turned out, gave his new master loyal and useful service.

Church hastened back through the woods to Plymouth to dispose of his prisoners. Then he hurried to the pond where, by the same tactics, he captured a group of Monponsets, members of a small tribe from whom the pond took its name. He continued these surprise attacks day after day, never returning to Plymouth without a batch of prisoners. Often, information of the enemy's hiding places came from stray Indians, whom Church called "ramblers."

Another practice of the captain's was to run a quick eye over a group of prisoners and single out those he thought would fight for the English. "I've chosen you," he would say, "because I think you will make good soldiers. Now, if you do not betray my trust, you shall be my men and will not be sold out of the country."

If the captives looked sullen and Church's own Indians called them treacherous dogs, as some did at times, he would clap them on the back and say: "Come, come, you look wild and surly, and you mutter, but that signifies nothing. My best soldiers were like that a while ago. By the time you've been along with me but one day you will respect me, too, and will be as brisk as any of my men."

What the captain said usually proved to be true. The captured Indians followed him and fought as bravely as the English troops. It was more to their liking to be on the winning side, and Church was the kind of commander whom the Indians, as well as the English soldiers, admired, and who quickly won their loyalty. His confidence was contagious, and he quickened his men with his own driving energy and his indomitable courage.

There came a day when Church led a small company southward, ranging as far down as Dartmouth on the coast of Buzzards Bay. Here they spent a night hidden in a thicket near the site of a garrison house. The next morning they came upon tracks that led in two directions to a large cedar swamp. On its outskirts, Church surprised and captured a group of Indians gathering whortleberries. There happened to be one among them who had come to know the captain during his stay on Aquidneck Island, and when the squaw saw him, she ran toward him, clapped her hands, and cried, "Church! Church! Church!"

From his prisoners the captain learned that the swamp was teeming with Indians, some of them Narragansetts and the rest Wampanoags. An old squaw told him he could find Philip deep in the recesses of the swamp. Church was brave, but he was not foolhardy, and he knew it would be disastrous to make an attack upon the swamp with so few men. So he gathered up his prisoners and returned to Plymouth.

There could no longer be any doubt that Philip had returned to the fastnesses of the swamps that were so numerous over most of the terrain of Plymouth Colony. With him had come, from the far reaches of the Nipmuck country, the remnants of his own people and of the Narragansetts. Why Philip had left the larger and more remote area of the Nipmucks can only be conjectured. Knowing that defeat was inevitable wherever safety might be sought, he may have come back to Plymouth Colony because of a homeward-yearning instinct that made him prefer to fight uncompromisingly to the end on familiar ground.

Hounded and harassed relentlessly by the English troops and their Indian allies, Philip knew that time for him was running out. He might dodge his pursuers by fleeing from one hiding place to another, but he could not hope to elude them much longer. And resistance had become hopeless. There were all too few warriors left to fight even if they had been well supplied with guns and ammunition. And the threat of starvation dogged the footsteps of the fugitive bands as they shuffled wearily from one refuge to another.

There were a few warriors and sachems who, like Philip, had determined to fight resolutely to the end no matter what the odds were against them. On July 27, Captain Samuel Hunting led a mixed force of English and Indians in a surprise attack upon the Narragansett sachem Pomham who, with a party of hungry warriors, had been discovered near Dedham. Although mortally wounded by a shot in the back, and unable to stand, the old chief found the strength to raise himself up on his knees and seize an opponent. Only a timely rescue saved the victim from being brained by Pomham's hatchet. Fifteen of the Indians were slain with their sachem, and thirty-four were captured.

On that same July day a different, and more familiar, scene was enacted in Boston. Citizens passing along the streets stopped to gape at the sight of Monoco leading about two hundred of his people in a mass surrender to the authorities. The Nipmuck sagamore had also foresightedly brought along the sachem Matoonas as a prisoner. This "malicious villain" had led some of the bloody raids against the English settlements early in the war, and Monoco, who was also wanted, had hoped to save his own neck by bringing him in. The authorities promptly marched Matoonas off to Boston Common, where he was executed by his Indian captor. By what foul means Monoco had trapped and bound the sachem was never revealed, but he succeeded only in delaying his own punishment by death.

This incident pointed up the element of treachery that was now still further weakening the crumbling resistance of the Indians and hastening their final defeat. To save themselves, many Indians were shamelessly becoming traitors to their cause. Betrayed by these renegades, Philip could no longer feel secure in secret shelters, for he did not know whom to trust among his own people or his own allies.

On the Sunday morning of July 30, two messengers came in great haste to Marshfield with intelligence for Governor Winslow. He was informed that a large number of Indians had been seen in the woods near Bridgewater. The governor lost no time in departing for nearby Plymouth where, upon his arrival, he called for Captain Church, who was attending services at the meetinghouse. Informed of the lurking enemy, Church needed no urging to march off in pursuit of them, and while Winslow mustered soldiers and Indian scouts, he raced to the storehouse to check provisions. There was no bread, so he and his man Jeffrey ran from house to house, collecting all the loaves the Plymouth housewives had on hand.

Shortly after noon the captain set out with his hastily assembled company. Toward evening they reached Monponset Pond, and since his men were exhausted by rapid marching in the heat of the day, Church gave the order to stop and camp by the pond for the night.

Early the next morning a small armed force from Bridgewater that had been informed of Church's coming marched out from the town to meet him. On the way the men encountered a company of Wampanoags and Narragansetts about to cross over Taunton River on the trunk of a large tree they had felled. A sharp skirmish followed, in which several Indians were slain, including Philip's old uncle Unkompoin. Church heard sounds of the firing as he marched along the northern edge of a cedar swamp, but being uncertain of the direction from which they came, he continued on to Bridgewater, where he learned about the encounter with the Indians.

At an early hour on the following day of August 1, Captain Church took up pursuit of the enemy with his own force and a number of Bridgewater men. They soon came "very still" to the leafy top of the great tree that spanned the river, and saw a solitary Indian on the opposite bank sitting on the stump of the fallen tree. His back was turned to them, and he seemed to be absorbed in his thoughts.

Church had raised his gun to fire when one of his Indians called out, "No, no—he is one of our men."

The sound carried, and the lone Indian on the stump turned quickly. In that instant he was recognized. It was King Philip! But the Wampanoag sachem was so agile that before Church or any of his men could fire their muskets, he had sprung up from the stump and disappeared into the woods.

Scrambling with all possible speed across the log, the captain and his company dispersed on the other side and scoured the area along the banks of the river and out in the forest. But the quarry they were so eager to capture had escaped. There were plenty of tracks, though, and the captain himself followed a path along which he overtook and rounded up a large group of Indian women and children.

Now and again the crack of a musket was heard. Some fleeing Indian who had made a vain effort to escape had been toppled by an English bullet. Many were killed, and all that day bands of captives were herded together on the riverbank and later marched off under guard to Bridgewater.

Trusted Indian scouts ranged far into the woods and returned now and again to report to Church when they found fresh tracks. The captain decided to follow what seemed the most promising of these footprints with a company of troops the next day.

Orders were given to march silently the following morning. Indian warriors were sent ahead well in ad-

vance of the main body of troops. Some in this picked
group returned in the afternoon with a large number
of Indian men, women, and children. It was from some
of these cowering captives that Church learned that
his Indians were leading him straight to Philip's lair—
to a swamp near Swansea where he had now sought
refuge with his surviving braves.

That night the English troops and their Indian
allies camped just within the boundaries of the swamp.
No fire, no noise—the captain's orders were strict. He
was stern in his talk to the captives, too, who were
bunched together. "There will be fighting in the
swamp tomorrow," he said, "and we can't spare any
men to guard you. If you value your lives, stay here
until the firing stops, then pick up our tracks and
come to us." Because they were mortally afraid of this
Mr. Church, they did as he ordered.

At dawn the captain sent two scouts to spy on the
enemy's position. But on the way they met two of
Philip's men who were out for the same purpose. The
Wampanoag scouts turned on their heels and fled with
such screeching and howling that before they reached
camp their chief knew he had been discovered. So it
happened that all the English troops saw upon plunging into the interior of the swamp were the kettles that
had been left boiling on the fires and the meat roasting
upon wooden spits.

There was no dillydallying on the part of the vigorous, alert captain. Orders, clean-cut and sharp, were

given at once. Isaac Howland, son of a prominent early Pilgrim, was sent on the run with a body of troops to the side of the swamp opposite that on which Church would take a group of soldiers. Working down toward the end, the two companies would form a wedge-shaped trap in which they hoped to catch Philip and his warriors. Another force was ordered back to the entrance to block off escape there.

As had been expected, Howland and Church came upon many Indians in flight at the end of the swamp. Instead of attacking their pursuers, though, the Wampanoags and Narragansetts simply appeared dazed for a moment. In that instant Captain Church spoke to them through an interpreter. "If one of you fires you are all dead men. You are hemmed in by a large army. Surrender and your lives will be spared." The stunned and beaten warriors gave up without lifting a gun or a hatchet, and Church appointed guards who herded them, along with panicky women and children, down into a little bowl-shaped valley outside the swamp.

Not all the Indians surrendered without a struggle, however. Elsewhere in the swamp there were skirmishes and single combats, and many of the enemy and some Englishmen were killed. The captain himself presently found himself in the midst of the firing, and had to fight for his life. Accompanied by two guards, he encountered three warriors, two of whom surrendered and were turned over to the guards, but the third Indian tried to escape. He was a large, stout fellow who had tied up his long black hair with a red ribbon, and a long rattlesnake skin hung down his back.

In the chase that followed, Captain Church overtook him and raised his gun to make an end of him. But the musket missed fire, and the Indian threw up his own firelock, which luckily also failed to go off, both guns having been dampened by the fog and the dew. Then the Indian took to his heels again, but he tripped on a grapevine and fell flat on his face. Before he could rise, Church was upon him, and killed him with a blow of his gunstock.

But the captain was not yet out of danger. Turning from the bloody business he had just finished, he saw Totoson, "flying at him like a dragon." Totoson was the Wampanoag who had murdered the women and children at Clark's garrison in cold blood. The St. George of that day's swamp fight would not have lived to fight again if his watchful guards had not "tried a shot at him and rescued their captain." But Totoson escaped.

King Philip had again managed to elude his pursuers, but Church discovered at the end of the day's fighting that he had two prize captives—the Wampanoag sachem's wife and young son, who was his only child.

Having no provisions left, and burdened with prisoners, Captain Church led his troops back to Bridgewater. Here the Indian captives were driven into the pound and placed under guard until the following day, when they were taken to Plymouth.

One of the captured Wampanoag warriors said to Church: "Sir, you have now made Philip ready to die. For you have made him as poor and miserable as he used to make the English. You have now killed or taken all his relatives. You will soon have his head, for you have broken his heart."

14   The Death of King Philip

A lone Indian deserter came into Taunton on August 6, and to gain favor with the English, revealed the location of an enemy encampment nearby where Weetamoo, squaw sachem of the Pocassets, lay hidden. Guided by the traitor, twenty Taunton men went there and took over a score of prisoners. Weetamoo escaped, but in an attempt to cross the Taunton River on a flimsy raft, she fell into the water, and drowned.

192

Some days later the squaw sachem's body was found, and her severed head became one more grisly trophy, which was exhibited in Taunton.

Captain Benjamin Church had hoped to rest for a few days after his return to Plymouth. Even a man as ruggedly strong as he could not pursue and fight Indians in all weathers and at all hours for days without end. His sturdy muscular body was beginning to sag from sheer weariness. But he had hardly eased himself out of his equipment when a call came to hasten down to Dartmouth where the enemy had been seen in the woods nearby.

Again the robust Indian fighter pulled himself together, strapped on his cartridge belt and bullet pouch, and with musket in hand departed for the Dartmouth woods with a company of Indians and English volunteers.

On the outskirts of the town, Captain Church broke up his force into small parties, and sent them off to hunt the enemy. That evening they returned to the appointed rendezvous with prisoners. It had not been a dull day. One group had brought in an Indian known by the name of Sam Barrow, "as notorious a rogue as any among the enemy." The Plymouth court had already given the order for his execution on the spot if he should be caught. So Captain Church at once passed sentence upon him: "Because of your inhumane murders and barbarities you must prepare for death."

Sam Barrow accepted his fate with stoical indifference. His preparations for death were simple and brief. He asked only that he be allowed to smoke a few whiffs of tobacco before his execution. As the smoke from the last puff on his pipe drifted away, one of Church's Indians sank the blade of a hatchet into his skull.

Then there was information from one of the prisoners about Totoson, the "dragon" who had fled from the captain's guards in the swamp fight. Having found his hide-out the next morning, Church's men easily captured about fifty Indians. But Totoson escaped again, this time with an old squaw. The Wampanoag leader fled back to what had once been a favorite haunt on the upland of a swamp between Wareham and Rochester. And here he brooded over the disaster that had befallen his people, the loss of all the members of his family, and his own perilous plight. "His heart became as a stone within him," and a few days later he died. The old squaw covered his body with leaves and brush, and then plodded off to Sandwich. It was from her that the English learned of Totoson's death shortly before she too died.

In Plymouth the authorities were impatient to bring about an end to the war with the capture of King Philip. So when Church returned from his expedition to the southern part of the colony, Governor Winslow persuaded him to press forward on the hunt without delay.

And once again the captain rode out of Plymouth, this time leading his company of hardy Indian fighters along the forest trails toward Pocasset. To all appearances it was deserted country, and after searching the woods without finding any sign of Indians, Church finally had his men ferried across the Sakonnet River to Portsmouth on Aquidneck Island. Here he left them camped near the landing, and with a few companions rode about eight miles down the island for a short visit with his wife, who at this time was staying with the family of Major Peleg Sanford.

The reunion was brief, for a few minutes after the captain's arrival, two horsemen came galloping up the road in a cloud of dust. They were Major Sanford himself and Captain Roger Goulding, the man who had rescued Church and his soldiers from the Indians in the Battle of the Peas Field the preceding summer. "Would you like to have news of Philip?" the two men asked in one panting breath.

Captain Church shot back the answer: "More than anything else!" In that moment his weariness vanished, and energy surged through him, invigorating every muscle.

Where was the Wampanoag sachem who for so many months had been a phantom of the forest? Knowing at last that he was doomed, he had, with what seemed like a sense of tragic destiny, gone back to Mount Hope Peninsula with the remnant of his loyal braves to make his last stand there against the hated English. He would die fighting in what had once been the stronghold of his proud race. He would fall on what he could still call his own ground—the neck of land that was all that remained of what once had been his father's widespread domain. Reflecting upon the utter devastation that had overtaken him, he must have wanted to die. But let the greedy, overbearing English come and take him, he must bitterly have mused with the old imperious lift of the head. He would never go to them and surrender. Betrayal, no less than the English troops, had dogged King Philip's fleeing footsteps. Betrayal brought him to his bitter end.

During those last days at Mount Hope, when his nerves must have been as taut as the great bowstring he once had pulled rigid, Philip had been angered beyond control by one of his warriors, who, knowing how hopeless their situation was, had urged him to surrender. Without a moment's hesitation, the infuriated chieftain had ordered him put to death.

An Indian who was a brother of the victim fled from Mount Hope, with hatred for Philip goading him to take revenge. He not only told Major Sanford and Captain Goulding where they could find the sachem of Mount Hope, but offered to guide them to his camp.

Captain Church knew that his great opportunity had come—the Indian corn was tall now; the stubby ears were almost ripe. Without delay, he and his men mounted their horses and were off at a rapid pace. Major Sanford and Captain Goulding galloped along with them, and they were soon in Portsmouth, where Church's soldiers awaited him.

The Wampanoag deserter was there, too, and he told the captain that he would find Philip on an up-

land in the north end of a miry swamp located at the
foot of Mount Hope. Church knew the place. How
well he remembered the late June day in 1675 when
the English troops had gone down into the neck to
search for Philip and had found it deserted—deserted
except for the eight murdered Englishmen whose severed heads stared down at them from the poles on
which they had been impaled.

The troops quickly clambered into the boats and
were ferried across the half-mile stretch of water to the
shore of Mount Hope Peninsula. Here they disem-
barked and, guided by the Indian deserter, hurried
on to the edge of the swamp where Philip had his
camp. It was now past midnight, and Captain Church
gathered his men around him and gave orders for the
attack at dawn.

Captain Goulding was given command of the key
group that would take the initiative in the assault.
They were instructed to crawl warily on hands and
knees up to the edge of the camp, and at daybreak to
launch the attack. It would, of course, bring the startled Indians leaping out of their shelter. While driving
them into the ambushes, Goulding and his men were
warned by Church to raise a great hullabaloo by shouting, for the waiting soldiers would have orders to shoot
anyone who ran silently.

The captain did not have enough men to surround
the swamp, but he placed those he had as strategically
as possible. Along one side, an Englishman and an
Indian were posted together behind each of certain

large trees at short distances apart. And on the other side, Church took his position with the remainder of his force.

At last all was ready. Laying his hand upon Major Sanford's arm, Captain Church said: "Sir, I have so placed them that it seems impossible for Philip to escape. We shall see."

Suddenly a shot cracked the eerie stillness of the swamp! For a moment Church thought some soldier's gun had been fired by accident. But no! A resounding volley quickly followed, then shouting and shooting from across the swamp. The captain waited, tense with anxiety and uncertainty. The firing had begun earlier than he had expected. What, he wondered, could have happened?

Presently, an Indian came running toward Church. He cried exultantly, "Philip is dead! I have killed King Philip!"

It was startling news, but Captain Church did not lose his composure. Calmly he ordered the Indian to keep silent. "Let no man know it," he cautioned, "until the swamp has been driven clean."

The attack had indeed begun sooner than anyone expected. One of Philip's warriors had roused from sleep and, as if sensing danger, had walked from the rude shelter into the dimly lighted swamp. It so happened that he gazed directly at Captain Goulding, who, thinking that he had been discovered, fired, and in the next instant his men poured a volley into the shelter. The only effect it had on the Indians was to

wake them with a start, for the bullets whizzed by
harmlessly overhead. In a moment all was confusion
as the warriors scrambled in frantic haste to escape
into the swamp. Foremost in the headlong flight was
King Philip. Dressed in short breeches and stockings,
he had seized his gun before bounding out, and now
he fled past Goulding's men and reached the woods
beyond his camp. But directly ahead a pair of Church's
men waited in ambush. Seeing the Indian racing toward them, they held their fire until he came within
range.

The English soldier shot first at a distance of a few
yards, but his gun failed to fire. A few more steps for
the fleeing sachem—one more breath of life—and a ball
from the Indian's musket crashed through his heart,
and then another just above it. For a split second the
tall, lithe body wavered, then crumpled, and King
Philip fell heavily face down in the mud of the swamp
with his gun under him. The Indian ran forward,
lifted up the head of the fallen chief, and cried,
"Philip!" Then he sped away to carry the triumphant
news to the captain.

The trapped warriors had run first toward the east
side of the swamp where Captain Church's men lay
in wait for them. Upon discovering the ambuscades,
they wheeled about, and most of them made their escape through the unguarded thickets on another side
of the swamp.

There was one among those that fled who tried to
halt the rout. It was an old warrior who must have

recalled for a fleeting moment the days of Indian glory when proud braves stood their ground and died, if that had been their fate, facing the enemy. He raised his voice above the shouts of the Englishmen, and cried out, "Iootash! Iootash!" (Fight! Fight!)

Captain Church's keen ears picked up the sound, and he asked the Indian beside him whose cry it was, and what was the meaning of his words.

"That is old Annawon, Philip's great captain," the Indian replied, "and he is calling on his men to stand fast and fight bravely."

This time Philip's warriors did not heed the battle cry of his great captain. And old Annawon, deciding that there was no honor in standing up alone to the victorious English, scampered away too.

By the time the sun came up on that Saturday morning of August 12, 1676, the swamp had been "driven clean." It did not matter that many of the enemy Indians had escaped. For King Philip lay dead, ingloriously sprawled out in the mud, forever stripped of his power to make war upon the English.

Captain Church called all of his men together around the shelter within which Philip and his warriors had been sleeping a few hours earlier. There he made the momentous announcement that the Wampanoag chieftain was dead.

When the tumultuous shouts of victory finally subsided, Church ordered his Indians to pull Philip's body out of the mire and to bring it to the upland. They obeyed with alacrity. Those who watched the corpse as it was dragged over the muddy ground saw nothing that reminded them of the proud monarch who had for years ruled the Wampanoags and agitated the leaders of Plymouth Colony. They saw instead "a great naked, dirty beast."

Standing over his mud-streaked body, Captain Church said to those who were gathered around him, "Since this beast has left many an Englishman to lie unburied and to rot above ground, not one of his bones shall be buried."

Then an Indian executioner was called, and ordered to give Philip's body the treatment of an English traitor. He not only came willingly with his hatchet, but he came with a little speech for the dead. "You have been one very great man, Philip," he said, "and you have made many a brave man afraid of you. But even so big as you were, I am now going to chop you to pieces."

The body was first decapitated and then quartered, and the sections were hung up in the trees. King Philip's head was carried triumphantly to Plymouth and set up on a pole. This greatest trophy of the war was on view there for over twenty years. Long, long after the once proud head had become just another bleached skull in which wrens built their nests, the Reverend Cotton Mather came one day to look at it. He could not resist wrenching off the jawbone and carrying it away. Later, when the eminent New England clergyman sat down to write a history of the tragic war, he referred to the incident in these words: "The hand

which now writes took off the jaw from that blasphe-
mous leviathan."

On a day late in that memorable month of August,
1676, Captain Church lay hidden in the bushes beside a trail that led into a swamp a few miles north of
Swansea. Crouched there in concealment with him
were two Englishmen and six friendly Indians. They
had separated from a larger company of soldiers who
were scouring the woods on Mount Hope Peninsula
and the area around Rehoboth in search of Indians
who had escaped with Annawon and who had been
foraging and preying upon the cattle and horses of
the inhabitants. Ten Wampanoag warriors had been
captured, but Annawon was not among them.

The one-time trusted counselor of King Philip was
known to be "a very subtle man, and of great resolu-
tion," who had often said that he would never be taken
alive by the English. And it was old Annawon that
Captain Church wanted as a prisoner more than any
other of the defeated warriors who were still at large.

Perhaps it was intuition that prompted the intrepid
Indian fighter to leave the main body of his troops and
conceal himself with a mere handful of men beside an
obscure path he had come upon. Whatever it was, it
brought him the opportunity for his most daring exploit, and the last for the illustrious captain in King
Philip's War. Happily, no blood was shed in this last
action; no gory trophies were carried off to be paraded
on poles. It was instead a moving incident of submis-

sion by an Indian whose nobility and dignity commanded the respect and admiration of the white captain to whom the surrender was made.

It might not have happened if Church had not decided to wait in ambush there beside the path to see
what would develop—and if an old man and a young
Indian woman had not come along from berry-picking
and been taken prisoners by Church. He soon made the
exciting discovery that the Indians were from Annawon's camp. When asked how many miles it was to
the camp, the young woman replied that she did not
understand miles. But she could tell the captain that
Annawon was in Squannaconk Swamp with a company
of about sixty men.

That information was enough. It was exactly what
the captain wanted to know, and when the old Indian
told him that they might reach the swamp by sunset
if they walked briskly, he recklessly set off with his
handful of Indians and two Englishmen, who had
readily agreed to go with him. Risky as the venture
was, Church looked upon the chance to capture Annawon and the Wampanoag braves as too tempting to
let pass.

Guided by the old Indian, the party approached
Squannaconk Swamp at sundown. They waited in the
woods until nightfall when they could proceed under
the cover of darkness. Church passed the time listening to his guide's description of the place where he
said they would find Annawon. It did not disturb the
captain to hear that it would be difficult to reach the

retreat of the old warrior, for he had overcome so
many obstacles during the hazardous months of fighting Indians that he felt confident he could hurdle
whatever lay ahead.

Annawon had escaped to a place of refuge that
seemed impregnable. Perhaps it would have been if
yet another Indian had not given the English aid.
Squannaconk was a vast swamp of nearly three thousand acres that lay to the southeast of Rehoboth. There
was an immense rock formation in it (now called
Annawon's Rock) that was surrounded by a scattering
of maple, beech, and birch trees, and such a tangle of
thorny bushes as made the approach to it difficult.

When night came, Captain Church and his men
crawled up a long, sloping ledge on the northwest side
of the Rock where the ascent was easiest. They did not
have to be too careful of their movements through the
brambles and over the rattling pebbles, for down
below in the camp an old squaw was vigorously pound-
ing corn in a mortar, making a great deal of noise. At
last they reached the top of the cliff from which they
peered down upon three separate camps, protected on
all sides by swampland.

They saw the Indians in the bright light of their
fires busy with preparations for supper. Pots and kettles were boiling, and hunks of meat were roasting on
the spits. Captain Church soon spotted the great Annawon with some of the braves around him. He also saw
that the Indians had stacked their guns against a rack

and covered them with mats for protection from the dew. This, he thought with satisfaction, was certainly a stroke of good luck.

Now the perilous descent began, with the men clinging precariously to small trees and bushes that grew in the clefts of the rocks. The old man and the young Indian woman went first, by command, clutching their baskets to look as if they had just come back from picking berries. Church crept close behind them, hatchet in hand, and his men followed one after the other.

By this stratagem the captain was almost in the midst of Annawon's company before he was discovered. And before the startled Indians had recovered their wits, he was standing beside the stacked guns. Annawon started up with the despairing cry "Howoh!" (I am taken!), and then dropped down to sit silently with an air of resignation.

The squaws and children cowered, and the warriors stood as if stunned. Captain Church, like a whirlwind that had suddenly blown up from nowhere, was putting the finishing touches on his coup. His own Indians had raced off to the other two camps to tell Annawon's followers what Church himself was now saying to the chief captain and his company: "If you resist or try to escape, you will be cut to pieces by my great army outside. Surrender quietly and I will see that you are well treated."

After the Indians had submitted, the captain's man-

ner became genial. "What do you have for supper?"
he asked old Annawon. "For I have come to sup with
you."

The broken old chief captain accepted defeat with
good grace. Which would Captain Church prefer, cow
beef or horse beef? When he said that he would like
some cow beef, the squaws scurried about getting his
supper ready. Seasoned with salt from a little bag that
Church pulled out of his pocket, the beef and the dried
green corn made a good meal.

After the captain had set his men to watch through
the night, he lay down near Annawon for the rest he
sorely needed. But he could not sleep, and he observed
that the old warrior was wakeful too. Some time late
in the night, Church saw him rise quietly and walk
off in the moonlight. He soon returned carrying a
large pack.

Surprising his captor by speaking for the first time
in good English, old Annawon dropped to his knees
and said, slowly and softly: "Great Captain, you have
killed Philip and conquered his country, for I believe
I and my company are the last that war against the
English. So you have now ended the war, and therefore these things belong to you."

Then the old chief captain pulled from his pack,
with what heartache only he knew, the things that had
been King Philip's—the regalia he had worn when he
presided over the rituals of his people. Annawon first
drew out a long, wide wampum stole, fringed with red
deerskin, and curiously and beautifully decorated with

black and white figures of birds, flowers, and animals. It was so long that when Church held it from his shoulders it hung down almost to his ankles. The wampum headband, which was taken out next, had two little flags stuck in the back, and there was a neckpiece with a pendant star. Last of the treasures were two horns filled with glazed powder, and a large red blanket.

For the rest of the night the old warrior talked about the happy times when he had been a young brave. He spoke proudly to his white captor of the wars in which he had fought against other Indian tribes when he had served under Philip's father, old Chief Massasoit. But he kept to himself the grief and the shame that undoubtedly filled his heart. He said no more about the terrible fate of his people, the once proud and powerful Wampanoags. Daylight came, and Annawon and King Philip's warriors left the Rock for the last time.

Epilogue

Soon after his exploit in Squannaconk Swamp, Captain Benjamin Church brought Annawon and the other prisoners to Plymouth. Before he departed for Boston to make a report to Governor John Leverett, he made a special plea that the authorities spare the life of the old Wampanoag warrior. But during Church's absence, the General Court in Plymouth condemned Annawon to death. He was accused of "torturing and murdering many English prisoners, which he could not deny," and he was shot and his head was cut off.

Captain Church had taken an active and important part in waging relentless war upon the Wampanoags and their allies, but after their conquest he had talked with Philip's "great captain," not as a bloodthirsty Indian, but as a human being with qualities of nobility—pride of race and achievement, bravery, loyalty to his sachem, fortitude, and a touching humility in defeat. So, upon his return to Plymouth, it was with sadness that Church looked upon the severed head of the proud old warrior.

It was not so quickly decided what disposition should be made of Philip's young son. Whether he should be executed or sold into slavery was widely debated, with the clergy taking a leading part in the discussion, and with few exceptions leaning toward severity of judgment. In a plea for mercy, the Reverend John Eliot cited II Chronicles XXV, 4:

The Lord commanded, saying, The fathers shall not die for the children, neither shall the children die for the fathers, but every man shall die for his own sin.

The boy did not die at the hands of an executioner in his homeland. He was sent out of the country to become a slave in the West Indies. With his departure from New England, old Chief Massasoit's last descendant disappeared from the pages of history, never to be heard of again.

Concerned as much for the conversion of the Indians to Christianity as for their humane treatment, Eliot had argued against the practice of condemning enemy prisoners to be sold into foreign servitude, but in vain. Most of the male captives were shipped out of New England and sold in the slave markets of the West Indies, and in far-off countries along the Mediterranean coast. This disposal of great numbers of prisoners had the advantages of bringing in money to help defray the cost of the war, of making available to the colonists large tracts of Indian lands, and of protecting New England from any more Indian trouble. The colonial authorities justified their action on the ground that they were dealing with traitorous rebels rather than with prisoners of war. King Philip's War, they reasoned, was a rebellion by subjects of the colonies—not a war between independent nations.

For captive leaders, and for those enemy prisoners who were found guilty of wanton acts of cruelty, the punishment was death. Although in most cases the death penalty was imposed after a trial in court, few escaped being either shot or hanged. Boston Common was the scene of many executions during the closing days of the war and for some weeks afterward. Eight Indians were shot there on September 13, and about two weeks later, Monoco, Sagamore Sam, and Muttaump—all notorious Nipmuck leaders—were seen being led through the streets of Boston to the gallows on the Common where they were hanged.

Even neutral Rhode Island meted out the death penalty to some of the Indians who had taken refuge within its borders. Four days after Philip's death, Quinnapin, the Narragansett sachem who had married Weetamoo, was captured, and after a trial in Newport was shot there on August 25. Indians were sold into slavery in the colony, too, but only for specified periods of service.

Such inhumane treatment of enemy prisoners is shocking, but it should be remembered that the New England colonists had experienced all the horrors of Indian warfare. To protect their homes and families from another uprising, they believed that the ruthless measures they took were both necessary and justified. There could be no justification for the shameful incidents of English atrocities, though. There was, for example, the burning of the wigwams, in which women and children were trapped, during the Great Swamp Fight. Barbarous practices were characteristic of the primitive natives; as civilized Christians, the English should not have been guilty of such flagrant cruelty.

The captured women and children, with the exception of Philip's son, were treated with less severity. They were allowed to remain in the colonies as bound servants of responsible families for a stated period of time. And Plymouth rewarded her loyal Praying Indians, many of whom had given invaluable service in the war effort, by setting up a special branch of government in 1682 with various provisions for their protection and welfare. In time these Christian Indians were absorbed into the white population by intermarriage.

There were numerous Indians who escaped the fate

of those who were captured, and those who voluntarily surrendered to the colonial governments, by fleeing across the Connecticut River to the west. Many of these fugitives found shelter with the Mohawks, and were later incorporated into that tribe. Some continued westward through the Iroquois country, and settled in what is now the state of Indiana. And still others made their way into Indian country far to the northeast. Along this northeastern frontier, Massachusetts fought with the Abnakis (also of Algonquian stock) for two years after the close of King Philip's War. In April, 1678, a negotiated peace brought the fighting to an end.

For the Wampanoags in southern New England, the war resulted in the virtual extermination of tribal life. A small remnant consolidated with the Sakonnets, and there are still a few Indians of Wampanoag descent in Massachusetts.

Before their decisive defeat, the Indians inflicted severe losses upon New England. A dozen towns were totally destroyed and many others damaged. The frontier eastward from Brookfield was pushed back almost to the coast. Hundreds of colonists lost their lives, and close to 600 men of military age were killed. The expenditure in money was enormous, and the economy of the colonies was disrupted, the fishing industry and agricultural production seriously affected, and the export trade almost ruined.

But the enterprising and industrious New Englanders recovered in time. For the conquered Indians there could be no recovery. The small number that survived the war and remained in New England had no choice but to acknowledge themselves the displaced subjects of the victorious English. And in a society in which English supremacy was unchallenged, most of the Indians sank to the low level of poor tenant farmers and hired servants. Philip, having sown the wind, had reaped the whirlwind that left desolation in its wake not only for his own people but for all the other tribes in southern New England.

The Wampanoag sachem lacked the strength and the ability to succeed in his plan to annihilate the white men and restore New England to the possession of the Indians. They were not organized for an all-out assault upon the settlements when the uprising began, and Philip soon lost control of the rebellion. There is no evidence that the tribes and their leaders who warred against the English were directed by a supreme commander, and no evidence, either, that Philip himself took a major part in the fighting. The conflict bears his name because he started it, and throughout the war he was the symbol of Indian resistance to the white men, but he was not the great leader that he was once assumed to have been.

Philip was a proud and sensitive Indian who bitterly resented the humiliations that the men of Plymouth imposed upon him, and this bitterness may have driven him, more than anything else, to plunge rashly into a war that doomed the tribes and brought about his own tragic death.

Almost the only remaining relic of the once numerous and powerful Wampanoags is the faint outline, in a clearing under the pine trees, of an Indian cornfield that was last tilled by the squaws almost 300 years ago. Farther down Mount Hope Peninsula, in what is now Bristol, Rhode Island, there is a simple granite marker that commemorates the fall of King Philip on August 12, 1676.

A short distance south of Mount Hope, Captain Benjamin Church lies buried in an ancient graveyard at Little Compton, Rhode Island. Brave soldier though he was, and a hero to the people of New England during King Philip's War, he is more happily remembered for his friendly relations with the Sakonnets and their squaw sachem Awashonks—and for the sympathy and understanding with which he listened to old Annawon's last recital of the glorious deeds of his people, the Wampanoags.

The echoes of the terrible conflict that pitted red man against white man have long since died away, but in the New England woodlands that both Philip and Benjamin Church knew and loved, the immemorial singing of birds can still be heard in the springtime.

Bibliography

Adams, James Truslow. *The Founding of New England.* Boston: Atlantic Monthly Press, 1921.

Bodge, George M. *Soldiers in King Philip's War.* Boston, 1906.

Bradford, Alden. *History of Massachusetts for Two Hundred Years (1620–1820).* Boston, 1835.

Bradford, William. *History of Plymouth Plantation.* Boston: Little, Brown and Company, 1856.

Burlingame, Roger. *The American Conscience*. New York: Alfred A. Knopf, 1957.

Bushnell, David. "The Treatment of the Indians in Plymouth Colony." *The New England Quarterly*, XXVI, 1953.

Church, Benjamin. *The History of King Philip's War*. Edited by Henry Martyn Dexter. Boston: J. K. Wiggin, 1865.

Drake, Samuel Gardner. *The Aboriginal Races of North America*. Philadelphia: Charles Desilver, 1860.

———. *The Old Indian Chronicle*. Boston: Antiquarian Institute, 1836.

Eliot, John. *A Brief Narrative of the Progress of the Gospel Among the Indians of New England*. Boston: Wiggin and Lunt, 1868.

Ellis, George W., and John E. Morris. *King Philip's War*. New York: The Grafton Press, 1906.

Hubbard, William. *A General History of New England*. Cambridge: Hilliard and Metcalf, 1815.

———. *A Narrative of the Indian Wars in New England (1607–1677)*. Boston, 1775.

———. *A Narrative of the Troubles with the Indians in New England*. Boston, 1677.

Hutchinson, Thomas. *The History of the Colony of Massachusetts Bay*. Boston, 1774.

Josselyn, John. *An Account of Two Voyages to New England*. London, 1674.

Leach, Douglas Edward. *Flintlock and Tomahawk*. New York: The Macmillan Company, 1958.

Lincoln, Charles H. (ed.). *Narratives of the Indian Wars, 1675–1699*. New York: Charles Scribner's Sons, 1913.

Mather, Increase. *A Brief History of the War with the Indians in New England.* Boston: John Foster, 1676.

Morison, Samuel Eliot. *The Story of the "Old Colony" of New Plymouth.* New York: Alfred A. Knopf, 1956.

Rowlandson, Mary. *Narrative of the Captivity and Restoration of Mrs. Mary Rowlandson.* Cambridge: Samuel Green, 1682.

Russell, Francis. "Apostle to the Indians." *American Heritage,* December, 1957.

Index

Wamsutta. *See* Alexander
War Council, 71, 142, 165-166
Warwick, 18, 136, 174
Watertown, 14, 135, 143, 144
Weetamoo, 22, 57, 58-59, 61, 70, 72, 78, 82-83, 150, 152, 154, 157, 211; death of, 192-193
West Indies, 68, 209; trade with, 20, 210
Wheeler, Thomas, 84, 85, 86, 95, 104
Wickford, 111, 112, 113, 114, 122, 123, 125, 126, 127, 136; negotiations at, 72

Willard, Simon, 91, 92, 95
Williams, Roger, 16, 17, 18, 27, 48, 139
Wilson, Thomas, 89
Winslow, Edward, 39, 180
Winslow, Josiah, 27, 40, 49, 50, 51, 61-62, 65, 175, 176, 178, 185; as commander in chief of expeditionary force, 110, 111, 112-115, 117-118, 122, 125, 126, 127-128, 129, 136
Winthrop, John Jr., 43

Young, Henry, 87, 89

DATE